Full Circle is a song, a ritual chant that helps us in the urgent return to our wild, expanded selves. Lyric essay, visionary art and verse combine as tools of the sorcerer, inviting personal transformation and invoking crucial planetary change. Universal images are lifted from the cauldron, the shared subconscious, danced into life as the incantations of the Mage, or as intricate line drawings bearing the secrets of roots and wings, of our place in the matrix of sentient Earth. These rhythmic elements combine into a song for the sacred interdependency of all life, for Gaia. *Full Circle* is a melodious romp, a thunderous pause, a return journey into the biological fabric, and the fabric of myth.

"The best of us have the thinnest veneer of civilization. The best of us instinctively see that the emperor has no clothes. The best of us understand the old ways, recognize that modern reality is merely a bad dream, see the waving prairie beneath the asphalt, feel the reverberations of ancient buffalo hooves through the night ground.

"In this book, you experience one of the best of the best. A man with primal energy running through him in bright bolts. A man too strong for this television society.

"The best of us don't belong here now. We're ghosts, too. Ghosts like the grass beneath the parking lot, like the hooves echoing through the centuries late at night.

"No, we do belong! Along with the ghost hooves and the sea of grass, we are Reality. It's the computer on which I write this that is illusion. We are at the last days of "civilization." Our drunken binge is about to end with a ninety-mile-an-hour crash against brick wall. Wolf's art and poetry is what is on the other side of that wall."

Dave Foreman
Author of *Ecodefense*
Co-founder of Earth First!

About the Author

The Indians of the Rio Grande watershed protected the underground shrines, the kivas, from which the clown-Kachinas arose to reinforce the sacred Earth-connection. Lone Wolf Circles lives the role of Kachina. An educator/activist of Viking ancestry, he re-inhabits an Anasazi ruin two miles from the nearest road. His sojourns into the cities, and to the killing fields of the environmental war, are devoted to the re-enchantment and re-empowerment of alienated humanity, with the goal of protecting biological diversity as the raw material of continuing evolution. Like the Kachina, Lone Wolf arrests preconception and trivialization, using the symbology of art, chants and music to extrude expanding awareness and determined response.

His "Deep Ecology Medicine Shows" weave ritual, dance, and rhythmic "talk" set to music in transformative performances. He also gives animated and informative presentations at schools, writer's conferences, media debates, environmental gatherings, public hearings and governmental agency conferences. Many of his benefit concert-rallies result in creative civil disobedience.

Lone Wolf's "earth lyrics" have been featured on several audio recordings and his work has appeared in various periodicals including *Earth First! Journal*, *Talking Leaves*, *Shandoka*, *5th Estate*, *Anarchy* and *Backpacker*.

To Write to the Author

We cannot guarantee that every letter written to the author can be answered, but all will be forwarded. Both the author and the publisher appreciate hearing from readers, learning of your enjoyment and benefit from this book. Llewellyn also publishes a bi-monthly news magazine with news and reviews of practical esoteric studies and articles helpful to the student, and some readers' questions and comments to the author may be answered through this magazine's columns if permission to do so is included in the original letter. The author sometimes participates in seminars and workshops, and dates and places are announced in *The Llewellyn New Times*. To write to the author, or to ask a question, write to:

Lone Wolf Circles
c/o THE LLEWELLYN NEW TIMES
P.O. Box 64383-347, St. Paul, MN 55164-0383,
U.S.A.

Please enclose a self-addressed, stamped envelope for reply,
or $1.00 to cover costs.

FULL CIRCLE

A Song of Ecology & Earthen Spirituality

—Lone Wolf Circles—

"A lyric journey through the wilderness and those wilds within ourselves. A journey through the artist's world view, to awareness, sensitivity, and the love and defense of our sacred, living EARTH.
A return to our primal selves, alive and free— FULL CIRCLE."

FIRST EDITION

Cover art and interiors by Lone Wolf Circles from original collage/drawings (incorporating turn-of-the-century illustrations in public domain) and limited edition lithographs, available signed and numbered from the author.

Library of Congress Cataloging-in-Publication Data
 Lone Wolf Circles, 1954-
    Full circle: a song of ecology and earthen spirituality /
 by Lone Wolf Circles. — 1st ed.
       p.   cm.
    ISBN 0-87542-347-7
    1. Nature—Poetry. 2. Spiritual life. 3. Ecology. 4. Nature.
 I. Title.
 PS3562.O4884F8   1991   91-24532
 811'.54—dc20   CIP

Llewellyn Publications
A Division of Llewellyn Worldwide, Ltd.
P.O. Box 64383, St. Paul, MN 55164-0383, U.S.A.

 Printed with soy ink on recycled paper

ACKNOWLEDGMENTS

Special thanks to:
- Carolyn Moran, who instigated many of these essays.
- *Talking Leaves*, Eugene's journal of spiritual ecology.
- The concerned staff of Llewellyn Publications.
- Barbara Mor, for insisting I "Turn it up!"
- Joanne Rand, John Drake, Terry Tempest Williams, Bill Szczech, Jim O'Conner, Bill Devall, and Robert "Bobcat" Brothers, for their untiring support of my work.
- Carlos Lomas, Dana Lyons, Mike Turk, Clan Dyken, the Stone Biscuit Band, Samba Joe Wheeler, and every musician who ever helped set these to song . . .

Other Books by Lone Wolf Circles

Waiting for Magician Morning: The Promise of Radical Ecology

Audio Recordings

Full Circle: The Vision of Lone Wolf Circles
Tierra Primera!: The Deep Ecology Medicine Shows
Tribal Jams
Wild Ones!

Forthcoming

Biognosis: Animal Teachers & The Re-Wilding of Humanity
Kokopelli Quest

TABLE OF CONTENTS

ILLUSTRATIONS

LONE WOLF CIRCLES

ARTIST'S PREFACE

"One can go through contemporary life fudging and evading, indulging and slacking, never really frightened nor passionately stirred, your highest moment a mere sentimental orgasm, and your first real contact with primary and elemental necessities the sweat of your deathbed."

—H.G. WELLS

"The purpose of art is not to represent the outward appearance of things, but their inner significance."

—ARISTOTLE

"Honor life. Without Earth, there is no Heaven."

—JOHN TRUDELL

Dedicated to those "two-leggeds" who suffered through my birth only to witness my painful response to a calling they could not hear—and to those special few who inspire me, including the "four-legged" and furry, feathered and scaled, green and growing . . . I couldn't make it without you!

Let's take a walk together through the Medicine Wheel, beyond dogmatic religion, sterile politics and anthropocentric (human-centered) reality. Shhh! Let's halt the commentary of our minds long enough to see more intensely, feel things in a deeper way. Abandoning the illusion of separateness, we become conscious and responsible participants in the landscape, in the sacred Medicine Wheel. "Deep Ecology" celebrates the sanctity and equality of *all* of creation, once the primary consciousness of our common ancestry.

It's true we are thinking, "New Age" beings, but our bones remain the moving strata of rock, a skeleton-antennae for the Earth's vibrations. Primeval passions swell like steaming lava in our expectant muscles, and by "pulsing" each other like the Mayans, we can feel those undammed rivers raging just below the surface of the skin. Our "higher being" is made up of selfless love and cosmic aspiration, but also soil, fluids, lust, sensation, and a joyous anger at the despoilers! Don't fear our natural, animal selves, or those mysterious colors of that tribal "past" watching for us in future-time. It is only the best of what we are that will survive.

While waiting for Magician Morning, I am at times a lens for powers greater than my individual self—ravaged by undiminished perception and the sharp edge of clarity. These powers arise like whispering thunder from out of my shamanic Viking roots and finally, the fertile, dream-laden grounds of my Anasazi pueblo home. Both the illustrations and the lyrics are set musically to the sonatas of echoing river, eagle's call, birdsong and the wistful wind of caves and kivas. The words were written to be performed to a diverse range of styles. Read-feel-dance them in this way.

I am at best a conduit, a humbled, human lightning rod for the strike of biological truths, burned into our very genetic code, carved into the helix of our primordial DNA. They have been found inscribed on the walls of prehistoric grottos, recorded in the fluid patterns of the universal subconscious, etched into our species' shared memory, painted in laughter, written in blood, tossed upon the winds of what-will-be . . .

Together, these pieces complete a song, a prayer for Mother Earth. See them as rhythmic reflections of the hidden source. Experience them as invitations to envision, inspiration to manifest that vision, and instigation to act.

Globally, as within, a tumultuous transformation is taking place. A great cleansing is coming, as foretold in the Mayan Calendar, the prayers of the Tibetans, the prophecy of the Hopi, and the promise of the feathered-serpent, Quetzalcoatl. A cleansing is coming! But beneath the ash, the ash of pavement, lies the certainty of seed:

The seeds of change, the seeds of the wild, the seeds of our relentless love. *Dare to be those seeds!*

Lone Wolf Circles
Land of Enchantment
Planet Earth
Late 20th Century

FOREWORD

by Barbara Mor

Lone Wolf Circles "grew himself up" on cement turf. Two decades earlier, so did I. Overnight bourgeois barrios, no-class cloned suburbs, tract houses in stucco blocks, a totally stripped earth: non-communities of endlessly driven, car-commuted people. A clean and tender land sold out, bulldozed, tackily replicated: pungent soil and sage replanted in generic streets and glaring miles of sidewalks no one walked. Along the grassy strip between sidewalk and curb, in the plotted and flagged real estate developments of my childhood, spindly young trees were regularly propped, one per lot, factory-made "nature" for factory-made neighborhoods. They never seemed to grow. Or, twenty years later, they'd thickened into that famous SoCall cartoon "scenery": public blobs of astroturf labeled "trees," "bushes," "plants." Ornamentally non-deciduous, dust-collecting, spaced-out rubbery green leaves corroded year-round by photocatalytic smog. A decorator landscape, created for drive-thru people. "The landscape of the future." We believed it. Easy to imagine an entire planet designed to look like a golf ball. A whole globe shiny, Newtonian, unreal as a country club golf course.

Young, on such a planet, you do not take "nature" for granted. It is everything that's missing. You know that it is missing. Flesh that is not metal. Smell that is not sprayed on. Hunger neither bought nor sold. Life that is not machine. The song of blood you know, hear, feel, search for everywhere, but cannot find. Or you find it, and are home forever: the epiphany of Earth.

A dry arroyo in the San Diego backhills, still pristine in the 1940s. Canyon stones smooth and round, heaped by ancient waters. A trance of grasshoppers rubbing fiery air with their sticks. I was four years old; my parents were sharpshooting in the backcountry. I wandered alone, my first experience of it. Gravity droned: the om-hum of sunbleached rocks, multi-dimensional insects, no-time. A rattler's suspended power in the ledge behind me. It pulsed, conscious and non-human, all around me. Suspended in every particle of dust and light, it pulsed. Rings of energy widened from me into the larger circle, dissolved, became it; simultaneous rings returned, continuous loops of energy—to be me. Each pebble, branch, chitinous filament, my body, existed discrete and clear; but resonating (aware of, being of) the larger presence. My consciousness, in that arroyo, was as it is now, fifty years later: earth lives, there are no boundaries. We are as mitochondria in the global cell; super-knots of conscious energy networking, like ganglia, the quantum/material/conscious body. Death, too, is that energy loop. The smaller body lies down and dies into the larger body; and vice versa. Wilderness, earth cycles: the quantum universe, a pulse in stone.

Suddenly, a shot rang out. Metallic sound ricocheted off rocky ledges, brush, sky. The deepest echo I've ever heard. A terrific crack opened the air, down through angles of light and steep stone, and through me. Stunned, different, I was shaped. I had encountered the real god of the world: every particle of earth was conscious flesh. No abstract god, paper theology, human-made ideology could ever equal or erase this experience. Real pre-human Being. Being primal and real.

Then a gunshot, repeated surreally like a terrible alarm clock that murders a dream. The shot was human. The echo was earth. The deep chasm that opened (I now know) was human history. A traumatic rip of the personal mind from the extant dream of Earth. I was four years old; yet all this was clear to me. Epiphany has no age. My life in lived years, and all human life now, is a return journey to that timeless/dreamtime/*alcheringa* consciousness. Hating, fighting (while living within) the machine-shot system that tore us from it.

Full Circle echoes my experience. Lone Wolf does not take the natural world for granted. He has lived the gross paving of paradise, watched humanoids "adjust" to the malterrain. Replanted in his birthplace, New Mexico, he knows the threatened glory and mute resistance of this earth. A poet, child and lover of earth, he does not forgive the mechanical cold-shot that daily, everywhere, tries to separate him from her body. Ontological wildness, a cellular memory, is his subject and his dream: he hunts for it, spirit and flesh, as our most important food. A warrior, Wolf lives to fight for Earth against the encroachments of robot machineries. He knows we all live and die within terms of ecospheric crisis: if not as warriors, then as trash, spit out as disposable things, through metallic teeth, into the dumps. A writer and powerful performer, he chants the ancient and urgent epiphany of this experience. As a friend, he asks us passionately to remember that his dream, poem, fight, and destination are ours also—to share or to lose.

Wildness is the optimum discipline. It works, and has worked from the beginning. Our best arts, technologies, systems, industries are still clumsy (mechanical) imitations of natural (magic) forms and processes. Wilderness is the last dance (than which nothing is more disciplined): a global, ceaseless, multi-dimensional interchange of energies and forms, simultaneously maintaining, destroying, (re)creating itself. Our best "gods" do only burlesque imitations of Earth's real act. Being more complex, more intelligent, more imaginative than: military order, intellectual constructs, or the logical interactions of machinery: *therefore*, wildness is endangered. As a butterfly up against a bullet. It is, of course, the civilized human who is deranged. Earth's only undisciplined creature is us. Not because we are "wild," but because we are mechanically/mentally separated from earthly process. Living out of nature's context, we are unnaturally stupid. In our stupidity, we think we are "free." We define "freedom" as our capacity to use, trash, and destroy the natural forms and energies of the world. Spelled out this way, the circularity of our stupidity becomes apparent: it is our own contextual body that is being used, trashed, destroyed. Our false "freedom" is suicide.

The definition of life is context. From before the beginning until after the end, human life is embedded in *non-human* context. Wholly functioning, interacting, conscious: larger than the universe, smaller than quarks: there is nowhere we can go to escape it. We are made of it. On earth, or off; rocketing "out" through telescopes or diving "inward" through microscopes: we cannot escape quantum/material/chemical/esthetic/experienced *process*. It is our spirit/body. Madness is the illusion of escape: the alienation of logical definitions, short-term systems, structural separations. I.e., a terrible mistake. Earth is not fooled by it. The consciousness of cosmic context and prcess is not fooled. Contemporarily, humans appear to rule earth, to ruin earth. But we only fool ourselves, only us: suicides, self-fooled.

Embedded in this relentless feedback organism: changes, evolutions, mutations, the endurances and disappearances of many lifeforms: the more disastrous/erroneous our misdcfinitions, the more instant and immense the feedback. We will get what we give (the process accelerates expotentially: it is, after all, great theater). Spewing poison into soil, air, water: we now swallow, breathe, bathe in poison. Dumping our shitty lifestyles into the ecosystem, we are befouled with designer shit. Turning the Earth into a golf ball, we become our own cartoon. Grotesquely defining our "freedom" as stupidity, greed, and waste: our best dreams, our finest works, our own progeny are bulldozed, pimped, and wasted. We give Earth the finger. Land, sea and sky hold up their mirrors. (Earth is a hyperreal poet. The bruises she exhibits are true poems, and mirrors.)

Such is the "his-story" of human "progress": a mass-story, holographically appearing on all screens: large and small, public and private, corporate and personal mind. Lone Wolf Circles knows (as we, also, *know*) this story is a sickness, a lie. Terminal, though profitable. A terrible mistake taught as "realism" in every school.

How do we pull back from this suicidal implosion: the *noir* fate of buffoons? We must rediscover the non-human context, remember the global multi-dimensional context: *put ourselves back into place.* To survive organically (as dreamers rather than robots), we must rebecome WILD. To rebecome wild, we must achieve spiritual clarity (the health of any wild animal): watchfulness, wisdom, and strength of heart, mind, and body. Not easy, in a human-mad world that rewards arrogance, denial, and weakness: where the most-fooled rule.

But we must do it. Books like *Full Circle* come to help. It is a document of poetic redefinition: a re-entry of the contemporary sensorium back into the trance/discipline of wilderness. A search for the rebirth of human wildness within the larger context of a threatened Earth. From beginning to end, Wolf's energy loop of intensely experienced movement and thought describes the retrieval of *us* by our own wild natures. Wild—not undisciplined, raving hordes of thrill-seekers, but *Wild:* ontologically of the earth, i.e. real and responsible animals. Spirit animals. Anasazi. Mayan. Viking. Celtic. African. Cro-Magnon. Zen.

Witch. We can all claim genetic authority for the return to our roots. "Poets were always pagans," Gary Snyder reminded us (pagan: of the earth). And all humans were once poets. Dreamers with/in the Earth. Conscious of the larger surrounding consciousness: its processes, needs, and visions. We don't need to invent a new "wild" style to rebecome what we *are.*

No longer tourists in other people's gods, on other people's sacred turf, tourists in our own skins (taking snapshots as substitutes for living experience; playing tapes of wind and waterfalls while the real world dies). We are unwilling to settle for "wilderness areas" worn like ornaments commemorating "nature" on an otherwise stripped and desecrated planet. We don't want to "vacation" in "nature" two weeks a year in an otherwise denatured world. We want to return to our roots in earth. We don't want to visit the "wild" on weekends. We want to *be* wild, forever.

We are (originally) disciplined, dreaming animals. Wild at the root (the bloodline to our Mother's belly). From many different, dispersed places we all arrive now at one place: between birth and death, what is truly worth living for.

The answer's in place. That place is Earth.

Barbara Mor
Co-author of *The Great Cosmic Mother*
(Harper/San Francisco 1987, 1991)

FOREWORD

by Bill Devall

If, as Percy Shelley said, "poets are the legislators of mankind," then we need more poets like Lone Wolf. We need poet-politicians who speak not only for humans but also speak for wolf, raven, coyote, for enchanted landscapes and wild places. We need poet-politicians who speak of the needs of the whole community—the land community.

Lone Wolf celebrates our relationship with other members of the land community—the soil, sky, plants, animals. He does not despair, as do many poets, at the gap between humans and nature created by modern culture. Lone Wolf finds a bridge across that gap based on his intuitive understanding of his own bioregion—New Mexico. He draws us into the will-of-the-land, the wilderness, as members of the land community, not masters of it.

Aldo Leopold, the great ecologist who defined the "land ethic," wrote that when we understand we are "plain citizens" of the land community, then an authentic "land ethic" can emerge. "The land ethic," he wrote, "simply enlarges the boundaries of the community to include soils, waters, plants, and animals, or collectively, the land." The land ethic ". . . of course cannot prevent the alteration, management, or use of these 'resources', but it does affirm their right to continued existence, and at least in spots, their continued existence in a natural state." Based on our acceptance of the "land ethic," we respect our fellow-members of the community and the community as a whole.

We could, of course, respect fellow-members of the community from a distance or out of fear of them. Or we can accept and respect them for what they are and embrace them as members of the community. Lone Wolf embraces rather than just observes or analyzes. His poems express what feminist writer Marti Kheel calls "unified sensibility." This sensibility ". . . is a sensitivity that must flow from our direct involvement with the natural world and the actions and reactions that we bring about in it . . ."

Lone Wolf's loving, erotic sensibility allows him to play on the ancient harmonies. He sings us into "magician morning," calling us to re-enter primal states-of-being-in-the-world. He seduces us away from the madness of modern, urban based civilizations and draws us into the "great silence," the way things are, the Tao. He opens the door of our consciousness and asks us to step out into the fields and mountains.

We could lock ourselves away in our houses in the city, bemused with our own despair, self-doubt, delusions. But we know, from the murderous and brutal experiments of the twentieth century—world wars, massive destruction, frantic projects built in the name of "economic development"—that when we lock ourselves in city consciousness we end up with nihilism and anomie.

When we open the door, leave our musty ideologies——marxism, capitalism, imperialism——and enter the mountains, we have a chance to form a relationship with the place within which we are dwelling.

In this house we call modern civilization, nature is only considered "dead matter," without consciousness or vitality.

When we leave our musty, human centered house to explore the fields and mountains, we realize that our real self, our authentic self is much broader and deeper than we imagined. Instead of loving our narrow ego, we begin, in the words of poet Robinson Jeffers, "falling in love outward."

But how can we take the first step out of our musty house? How can we rediscover the enchantment of the earth? We must become, as anthropologist Loren Eiseley said, our own "last magician."

In his collection of essays, *The Invisible Pyramid,* published in 1970 and containing his testament of his own ecological self, Eiseley concluded that humanity has crossed the first sunflower field of nature into the second field of culture. Now, in the late twentieth century, the power of our technology and the nihilism of our consciousness has brought us to the brink of disaster, to the possibility of nuclear warfare. Humanity faces a magician shaping its final form:

". . . a magician in the shape of his own collective brain, that unique and spreading force which in its manipulations will precipitate the last miracle, or, like the sorcerer's apprentice, wreak the last disaster. The possible nature of the last disaster the world of today has made all too evident: man has become a spreading blight which threatens to efface the green world that created him . . . the nature of the human predicament is: how nature is to be reentered; how man, the relatively unthinking and proud creator of the second world—the world of culture—may revivify and restore the first world which cherished and brought him into being."

The job of the poet, in this situation, says Lone Wolf, is to help us be our own last magician, to sing us into a glorious "magician's morning."

Lone Wolf calls us to listen, be quiet, sit in the middle of the great silence—vulnerable, receptive, open. Our suffering is very much with us as we sit in the middle of the killing fields where so much biological diversity has been murdered by advancing modern civilization. But if we are alert—very alert—patient, attentive to the way things are, then Pan will return from his hiding place in the forest and teach us the will-of-the-land.

Bill Devall
Co-author of *Deep Ecology*

THE MAGICIAN

In the smallest, furtive lizard lies coiled a great dragon. It gives their eye that special glimmer and, like a tight spring, empowers their explosive movement. In the tiniest of fledgling sparrows, lifting their fragile new wings from within, are the ancient leathery arms of the pterodactyl, creating a rush of wind that whispers from the past, "Fly, fly . . ."

Inside the dullest, most distracted and frightened human being exists a magician, squatting, knees to chest, on the balls of bare feet. He rests, always ready, while noiseless lightning stirs the cauldron of the mind, activating ether for the alchemy of the creative process. It is Medicine Woman, Currendara, harboring genetic truths deciphered from the blood. It's a shamanic warrior, prepared to interpret the bones of the buffalo, the swoop of the raven and the clear message of the green-growing beings.

I want to help you get in touch with the Merlin inside you, that Druidic-Viking-Slavic-Oriental medicine man/woman who resides in us all. Every race of two-leggeds has in its primitive heritage the immortal truths we've heard voiced from Lao Tzu to Black Elk. They speak of the truths of the spirit, the freedom of humankind, the sacredness and equality of all life—truths civilization had to suppress for us to devolve into the pampered despoilers of this planet.

Even the most pitiful human, physically weak from an urban lifestyle, mentally slowed by reliance on leaders and priests, TV and computers, distracted by the endless parade of meaningless new toys—has a primeval savannah inside him. So-called civilized man developed conceptual reality as a barrier for protection from the unknown; but the same barriers block sight of those infinite grasslands of human potential.

1

Listen to the magician inside you! It is a Brujo pointing with sharpened antelope bone to the vastness beyond contrivance. The real spirit of our species is hunting and gathering on Walkabout, way out there, on that savannah within . . .

Ignorance means deliberately *ignoring* the unused senses. Ignoring genetic and cultural lessons, ignoring the cries of other species backed up against the wall, ignoring the sparks that arise from the cauldron of our mind. Sparks that, in their wild, individual dances, seem to say to us, "Fly, fly, fly!"

Pan

Don't think of me
when you think of permanence.
That's a different animal,
you know.

Think of me
when you think of magic
of the swelling tides
that power our naked souls.

I am a changeling.
I love the feel
when polished horn
spirals from my skull.

I love the feel of fur
as it grows from my body.
Full-moon surge,
of course!

But even in faintest starlite,
bending to smell
your damp tracks,
I am filled with power.

The power of wild!

Why I Hurry

To all the forests I've had relationships with,
touched skin to skin, only to part.
I never forgot you, your many moods
and many ways of touching me.
But life is so short for knowing you all,
and they would steal you from me—
so fast . . .

To all the rivers I've known, intimately.
Touched skin to skin,
water-being to water-being,
only to part.
I never forgot you, your many moods
and many ways of touching me.
But life is so short for knowing you all,
and they would steal you from me so fast . . .
And to all those women
I've been privileged to love,
touched skin to skin, only to part.
I never forgot you, your many moods
and many ways of touching.
But life is so short for knowing you all,
and they would steal you from me—
so fast . . .

But at night, my mind becomes
a summer meadow.
All the vanished forests of the world
line its edges.
Every undammed creek and river
courses through.
All the extinct animals return to play.
Sometimes furry and four-legged,
sometimes naked with two,
I tumble through this meadow,
ever watchful for signs of the one song
that is the sum of women's many voices—
the voice of Mother Earth!

And the suddenness of morning reminds me
that life is so short;
that like Indian-proud women,
the rivers and forests are now rare.
And they would steal you from me—
and they would steal you from us—
so fast . . .

LA TIERRA

Barefoot walk.

Compelled to stop, push naked, probing toes into sun-warmed gravel, lean forward as the grassy knoll softly gives like a rib cage to the weight of my pressing knees. Myriad winged insects dance out their species song below.

Twirling silken sweet grass between my fingers, all realization of time vanishes down those invisible tunnels that bring the wind to our ears. It is a piece of her delicately braided hair my fingertips rejoice on! The connection made, I suddenly see all the places I have never been, creatures strange and familiar, the resplendent whole made visible to my pitiful humanoid eyes.

La Tierra es mi querida.

The Earth is my lover.

Walking, it is easier to feel her . . .

Her cloak is the rich tapestry of life, from microbe to field mouse, honeybee to buffalo, creeping-crawling-leaping-flying-bursting from their woven matrix. Awareness brightly lit with lizard luminescence, plucks my speech like flies from the air, dumps me on the fleshy cause of interminable wetness.

Walking, it is easier to hear her . . .

Every wild fruit rolls out her pores. Tides pound in blood-red grapes, her moon pulling their fluids hard against their giving inner walls. It is the sound of waves crashing on rocks where fruit meets stem, drumming their message of fullness down electrified vines. Their message is translated in her heart, along with timid emanations trickling down the roots of mountain flowers, and the barrel cactus' slow sucking of the centuries.

La Tierra es mi madre.

The Earth is my mother.

In her center rivers circle in, like coyote circles before resting in scented nest. The rivers are nose to tail here, smelling each other. Like sheets of opal, what you might think are lakes are the openings to the imaginations of mountain-bred children. We make just the right music to get in, rolling beach stones together in our palms, the anxious mating sounds of endangered species, the flapping of butterfly wings on the horizon . . . Unshakable view of the sacred . . .

Sacred walking . . .

COMING TO OUR SENSES:
The Art Of Ecoception

How we perceive the world—see, hear, taste it—influences how we think it, and therefore how we live it. Our collective impact and most societal constructs are the products of flawed perception.

One significant weakness is our concentration on minutia rather than the whole, focusing on details at the expense of the overall composition. In the process of painting pictures, I noticed that intricacies executed up close appear to create an imbalance when viewed from a distance. We have a great deal of our identities invested in that work-in-progress we call civilization. We find it difficult to step out of our cultural bias for a moment, to step back far enough to recognize the "life out of balance" that the Hopi pronounce "Koyaanisqatsi."

We have divided our experience of the timeless "now" into exacting fragments. Some days seem like weeks because the reality of experiential time will never conform to our pat measurements. Primal perception is in revolt against the modernist perspective. We have divided our visual plane into calibrated "sets," manageable, exclusionary zones of focus. They are at once evaluated and prioritized according to their immediate relevance to the narrow self.

Step outside and try this artist's trick. Arrest the cerebral prattle and look ahead of you. Now, with a newly quieted mind, try relaxing your eyes until they blur slightly. At this point, every element within our sight is situated on a common focal plane, reintegrated into the composite whole. The picture becomes complete, and "imbalances" in our human-scape become as obvious as imbalances in hue or value in an oil painting seen from afar.

Taken out of its literal context, you will find this technique still works. Walking down the paved streets of our metropolises, we typically practice a kind of tunnel vision, as though peering down a tube a few feet in diameter. We see only in the direction we are hurrying, just far enough ahead to react to obstacles, close enough to watch where we place each step. We ignore the imbalance, the stark oppressiveness of the power lines, the towers of commerce looming overhead like giant gravestones. Driving through national forest we focus on the pavement in front of our speeding vestibule, somewhat aware of the row of trees left standing as a scenic resource alongside the endless miles of highway. What we fail to see is the greater picture, the thousands of acres a few yards farther from the road, where all growth has been clearcut logged until only barren, eroding hills remain. To see the imbalances of a world gone awry, as well as to hear the still-perfect harmonies of remnant nature, we need only slow down, step back out of dialogue, and relax our eyes. A totality of experience joins the completeness of eternal present-time, all elements of this artistic composition reunited, in balance with each other again.

Our analytic systems plague our other atrophying senses as well. We subconsciously and automatically categorize audio input. We select one thing to hear at a time, tune in to one person at a time while blocking out the rest. Most sounds are relegated to background noise until our mental computers deem them threatening, curious or alluring. This selective awareness may serve to protect us from the sensory bombardment of our maddening urban environments, but the accumulative result is a flattening of experience and the impoverishment of our existence. It is akin to watching a ballet but only seeing the elbows of the dancers, or attending a symphony, hearing only the violin.

In contrast, other animals enter a scene instantly cognizant of every sound, seeing every movement-nuance-shape in the form of a composite. In this way, they are more fully present, more actively alive than we are, far more connected to the contiguous world through vigorous, sensual contact with it. Our limited perceptivity trivializes the magical world as it secularizes and marginalizes our selves.

A complete opening up of the senses obfuscates our imagined boundaries, contributes to real oneness with the Earth by dissolving the artificial border between self and environment. Reclamation of our senses is an immersion into our complete, wilder selves, and consequently into our greater self—into the inclusive, planetary body. It is interfacing with the sacred crucible, the cauldron of tests, the womb of creation.

At the atomic level there is no real demarcation point between the rock and soil, the soil and the tree, the tree and the air it breathes. All of creation is permeable, exchanging molecules through porous membranes, swapping atoms in symbiotic transfusions of vital energy. To be "at one with the all," to be in the "flow" means to consciously, wordlessly, deliberately access this perception, this universality. Self-realization, in the highest sense, involves our corporeal permeability—inundated by the sights, sounds, smells, tastes, textures and temperatures of aroused life.

We are taught to segregate experience from childhood on. The insulation we develop to protect ourselves from distress or distraction muffles our experience and deadens our lives.

It's difficult, after years spent pulling curtains closed on cubicles of compartmentalized reality, to begin opening the curtains and receive (re-perceive) the eager stimuli flooding in. It's *excruciating*. Let's examine this word. "Ex" means intense, and "cruciating" means to allow crucification. In other words, voluntary exposure to the intensity of experience. Excruciating life, wondrous life! A fete of animal sensation.

We can be as a lake is, silently receptive, open to those lashing rains that fill it past its temporary and penetrable boundaries, redefining itself as it encompasses the landscape and absorbs it into itself. We can be like that, our sensory organs open to the intensity of spontaneous input, transcending those illusory limits that once defined who we are, inundating the "outer" and the "all," assimilating the rest of the world into this broadest realization of "self." By daring to really feel, to really actualize each receptive sense, we are set free. Like that wilderness lake, we spill gleefully over the banks. We are released. We are fulfilled.

This expansive ecoception affirms the intrinsic and equal value of every species of plant and animal, as well as the rivers and mountains we labeled "non-life." Once we envision everything within an integrated and continuous field, we see that to remove any single element diminishes the whole, thereby impoverishing both viewer and spirit.

What we are calling ecoception is the perspective of all life—except for civilized humankind!

Civilization developed in a linear regression that paralleled this narrowing of perception. We practice a neurotic obsession with finite particulars to the neglect of an indivisible whole, the *tout ensemble*, the crucial context. Our intricate creations function as planned with their limited reference, but like pieces from dissimilar jigsaw puzzles, they fail to mesh with the greater patterns. They no longer resonate with the harmonic matrix that gave them birth. True only to their own abstract and inflexible laws, our social and technological systems reinforce the alienation at the root of our "fall from paradise." We service the narrowly defined at the cost of our totality. We are like adolescent children of the new-machine, listening to commercials on transistor radio headphones while strolling through the woods, oblivious to nature's sonorous celebration.

The "adept," the shaman, eschews the modernist opus, not to march to the beat of a different drummer, but to rejoin a sacred dance of interpenetration and communion, set to the inexorable heartbeat of the living Earth. Ecoception is organic perceptivity, the perception of the complete, ecological self. It is the sensory exploration of ourselves and of Gaia, the planet-body. "Eco" means household, coming from the Greek word "Oikos." Each of us evolved with the capacity to act as the Earth's sensors, and to protect this hallowed house.

All of life invites us to chance the excruciating intensity of uninsulated experience: the view from home.

THE ENCHANTED WEB

It's exciting! I now know the secret of reaching out to the sun!

Joan Halifax speaks of the invisible threads that connect all shamans to one another. And connects each of us as well—the Earth People. The last magicians on whose souls rest the responsibility to invoke a new/old Earth, an Earth once again wild and free, an Earth once again green and growing, diverse and inspirational. Our liturgy is our love. Our dogma is our action. Spiritual Warriors, *defenders*. Rare conduits of clarity in a time of blinding noise and neon. We have returned to the great mystery, humbled by our place in the awesome harmonic whole. Determined to dance out our individual dances, without ever losing step with the greater choreography of which we are a part.

I'm excited! The energy is incredible. The global metamorphosis is not time to hide in pat relationships, pat ideas—no time for the "I've done my part" rap. The transition, no matter how bright, demands us to look! Unwavering vision. Unwavering intent. I'm excited! Because I sense more acutely than ever our connection to one another, and to the grateful life forms we protect. It's not really a thread that connects us after all, but strands of an enchanted web. We can feel each other from great distances, through delicate vibrations. We have only to reach out now, along these fibers—over roaring rivers, under growing tree energy, over flying bird energy—to touch the source, *through* this warp and weft of interconnected consciousness. We form the voluntary fabric of our shared destinies.

Yes, I am excited! I stand as if barefoot, out of breath, staring wide-eyed at the wonder of the magic exploding before me. I hear the high-pitched cries of the clear-cut forests, and I feel the joyous anger of knowing, at long last, what to do about it. Each fateful moment unfolds, not like some burdensome movie plot, but as volcanoes unfold, thunderous and immediate. Demanding our undivided attention.

I'm thrilled because some of us are re-enchanting. Some of us are earning the right to be called "sensitives" again, reintegrated into the living, breathing flux. I'm thrilled because as loving and responsive Earth Warriors we redeem our species in the eyes of Creation, we further the real evolution of our species, and ultimately verify our true personal worth.

No, we are *not* the Universal Weaver that sets design rules for the patterns in rock, the flow of fire, the perfect twists in peach-colored sea shell. But we *are* the voluntary magic that fills the loom, reaching out again in a struggle to save the planet. Reaching out again for each other. Reaching down deep again to grasp the very heart of the sacred Mother, and thereby grasping understanding. This is the essence of my secret. Reaching down to the innermost heart of the Mother Earth, and thereby reaching out to the sun!

THEY LEFT US THE DESERT

If the desert is anything, it is wild, and the wilds are pure magic. This is the paramount quality of the untamed and untrampled. Any practice or attitude that diminishes this magic is guilty of the worst imaginable crime: that of imposing dullness and sameness on a world of diversity and change. While the mountains are for the most part covered with a layer of aspiring and perspiring Boy Scouts, the majority of our national forest elbow to elbow in the new "outdoorsman," much of what we call desert lies untouched, raw, a stark and invigorating expression of wildness, awakeness, and freedom.

The polluting Winnabago drives on, past the poem of the shifting sand I would share with you, each granule a different combination of shapes and hues. Past the elements of a different time: smug, hidden lizards making their dinosauric movements unseen. Past the twisting patterns of a thousand kinds of cactus and their thorny blossoms, past the intricate grain of salt cedar, shedding its fur for the nests of birds and rodents. Now, the stillness of the sparrow hawk sets in. Next, the arresting movement of the dry grasses, touched by power, dancing like the upraised arms of angels in the sweet smelling breeze. Finally, the sun moves into the rocks, emanating a warmth of pink and purple, the last rays falling upon the calendar engravings of the long departed Anasazi, marking the ceaseless rotation of the seasons. Boulders spit out of volcanoes when reptiles reigned supreme. A sherd of painted pottery here, drifting mesquite leaves there. Inscribed on the walls of the wind and water-cut caves is Kokopelli, North American Pan, universal role model. What appears as a hunched back is the internalized burden basket, containing not only the mistakes of history, but also the weight of humanity's potential. Still, with ever present erection, he continues to play the flute, dancing the world into existence with the fertile rites of Spring.

It would seem the immigrant tumbleweed waited for dusk to cross the alien road, where a sidewinder now absorbs its unnatural black heat. The broken white line fades as the stars open up like receptive lovers (never seen so many!), above the smooth glide of fox and owl.

They've left it for us; for the likes of cactus and coyote and me! Same as the hard-to-get-to canyon at nine thousand feet, it's a vast expanse of desert where you can feel the silence clear down to your bones. Find in the sand a path to your soul.

The secrets within the secret. Healing herbs. Peyote. Mullen. Yucca. Wild foods like coletus. Prickly pear. Piñon, arroyo and gully, spring seep and the tracks of the quail, all stories for those who can read them; the *real* things to learn. The sands turn over, perpetually, like the softened pages of Aldo Leopold's journal.

Walk carefully through each lesson. Avoid the stinging cholla. Watch for blue quartz and fire agate. Shy rattler. Ancient spearhead pointing the way towards awareness and awe. Walk quiet, so as to hear the music. Call of the ground squirrel, the chorus of weeds, the yips and howls you can follow but will seemingly never get closer to. The warm desert wind whistling through the dried cholla's skeleton, and then through yourself. Walking as message.

And then, walking as *massage*. Touching the Earth with the responsiveness of love. Unhurried steps in the hush of night, as if something, indeed, were sacred! Cottonwood roots are exposed in the dry wash, a curving waltz of tree tissue, reaching, stretching toward life-sustaining water, towards the source. *Become* the roots. Don't balk, let your muscles be the flowing wood. Tap the source. Bare your face to the touch of the moon like the surface of a lake. Bare your face to the unrelenting passion of the sun, like weathered bark. Close your eyes and let fall the walls of your mind! Leave the gates open, your consciousness spread out on a boundless valley. The cities are forgotten in this realm of the gods, and all anxieties vanish to a tiny point on the distant horizon, many days walk behind you.

But, no . . . let's tell them instead about the desert's loneliness, alkaline water, ghosts of the past, heat-seeking scorpions, scarcity of gas stations and commodes, the increase in rabid skunks . . .

After all, we have a responsibility.

Dreamsmells Of Coyote

We listened to the imploring call of the loon,
    ripple of water
    anxious panting of our mates.
Then, our ears are pared off at the skull,
    the rest of our bodies left behind—
    not required for bounty, for bounty . . .
We smelled the still-living flesh of our quarry,
    first-budding wildflowers
    salty air a thousand miles from the sea.
Then, our noses are shoved into the pavement,
    speeding shiny metal—
    never stops, never stops . . .
We tasted the sweet flesh of running hares and
    farmer's melons,
    morning brook's bubbles
    pungent love's juices.
Then, our tongues are removed
    by rusty barlows in callused hands,
    nailed to juniper posts—
    rancher's joke, raven's snack . . .
We felt the mud rush up between our toes
    in pursuit of sensation
    in celebration of life.
Then, our paws are removed and
    skins stretched, bodies uneaten,
    behind the barn—
    beneath the relentless sun, relentless sun . . .

We saw mating elk and fed on the
    bloodied grass,
    watched seasons change
    drank the colors of sunset.
Then, they set traps that sprayed cyanide into
    our too-eager eyes,
    running blindly into rocks—
    unable to breathe, unable to breathe . . .
We dreamt of wet noses and full moons,
    sweaty fur, playful bites
    family, love and eternity.
Then, our heads full of dreams are
    bashed with clubs,
    dreams unleashed like circling wind—
    freed to remake themselves . . .
We are dreams flying again in
    scampering rabbits,
    loving artist's fingers
    howling across these sheets of treeflesh.
On and on, to the forever world
    we never really leave,
    the last laugh—
    the dreamsmells of coyote . . .

The Job Of Poetry

Let me take you for a moment
from that frantic video you call "reality,"
a contemporary hit co-authored by fear.
Noise and commotion pulled up around you
like the false security
of an electric blanket;
encircling you like covered wagons
against the intense
uncertain potential of nightfall,
of our wild, unchained dreams.

Let me take you for a moment
to the shadow-lined corridors
between Tamarac and Aspen,
down those thorny, berry covered tunnels
that lead to your naked wild soul.
Silence will stalk you there,
coming closer even as you stop to listen.
Another step or two,
and it will reach out and touch you.

There is no winning without such struggle.
There is no freedom without such danger.
Shaggy hair hangs over your eyes here,
as even your tracks are transformed—
larger now, deeper,
with a hint of claws.
It is the job of my poetry
to take you there.

GREENFIRE:

Leopold And The Wilderness Ethic

On the windward side of State Highway 180, halfway between historical Silver City and the frontier hamlet of Reserve, there's an undeveloped rest-stop common to those sparsely populated stretches of New Mexico's secondary roads. Braced by a concrete footing against the prevailing storms, a small bronze plaque honors a most *un*common man. Here stands the sole monument to the great naturalist Aldo Leopold.

Sunset is the best time to experience the wonder and awe he described. It's the perfect light for rediscovering the aura of magic that infuses things wild and free with an undiminished character and color. There's never very much traffic at this hour. The sound of an occasional pickup truck seems distant and wavering at first, passing in a crescendo, then fading out into the twisting turns of Little Dry Canyon and Soldier Hill. Few drivers ever stop, and fewer still walk off the

gravel parking area to the memorial with its twin forty-four caliber holes. The brief text commemorates Leopold's efforts to protect his favorite mountain range, with its dramatic scenery and its diverse plant and wildlife. It was at his urging that the Forest Service set this primitive area aside, to be saved from the destructive effects of development for all time. In 1924, some forty years before passage of the Wilderness Act, the Gila became the first roadless area in the United States so designated.

Facing east from the plaque, we watch the play of changing hues on these primeval children of volcanic activity, the mountains he loved so personally and so deeply; from Mogollon Baldy to Bear Wallow bathed in pink, then purple as darkness falls. Their greatness lies not only in their explosive chroma and sheer, towering sides, but in their sense of peculiar antiquity. They appear as geological elders holding council, standing like eternity in the face of the clouds' maddening rush. It is an opportunity to feel humbled by something that is greater than our individual selves, yet something of which we are an integral and permanent part.

He taught that we are, like all of creation, an inseparable part of a living biotic community. He insisted that as the most prolific species, humans must consciously develop ethics defining how we interact with the rest of life on what he perceived to be a vital, breathing planet body. "That land is a community is the basic concept of ecology, but that land is to be loved is an extension of ethics." Leopold was one of the first modern writers to address our relationship to the remainder of this land community. He asks that we go beyond our roles as thoughtful custodians to a sensitive interaction that recognizes an objective, *intrinsic* value shared equally among life forms. The tenets he so fervently espoused find new expression in "Deep Ecology," a new spiritual philosophy combining fresh considerations of morality with conservation practice. He suggests that every species, every element of nature, has a right to flourish and evolve, free of even our *best* intentions.

The word "anthropocentricism" was coined to describe an exclusively human-centered orientation. It refers to measuring the significance of each thing in terms of its resource value (whether for logging, mining, or scenery) to the one dominant species: humans. With "Deep Ecology," no species or habitat is any less valuable, even if no human eye ever feasts on its special beauty. For Aldo, a seemingly ordinary pond of overlooked desert was just as beautiful, as crucial to the inextricable web of life, as worthy of our protection as pristine shorelines or the imposing grandeur of the Gila. He believed that to really "see" magnificence is as much a measure of the beholder as of the view.

"There are woods that are plain to look at, but not to look into . . . The taste for country displays the same diversity in aesthetic competence among individuals as the taste for opera or oils . . ."

Aldo was born in 1887, a full quarter century before New Mexico statehood, the same year Benjamin Harrison ran the presidency, Nikoli Tesla perfected the electric motor and Sir Arthur Conan Doyle wrote the first Sherlock Holmes story. He grew up back east in the last decades of a century marked by the creeds of dominion over creation and "Manifest Destiny." The illusion of endless lands had faded by its end. The finite forests, wild game and clean rivers of the United States had once seemed inexhaustible. But by now, the eastern forests and southern hardwoods were reduced to a shadow of their original selves, and hundreds of species joined the list of the newly extinct.

The bison were largely gone, the grizzlies and the wolves extirpated for the sake of forest-grazing livestock. A European penchant for a certain

felt hat brought about the decimation of vast populations of North American beaver, while eastern-seaboard fashions threatened the beautifully feathered waterfowl. The turn of the century was ripe for the creation of an Aldo Leopold, a John Muir, and finally a president that was an enthusiastic outdoorsman and conservationist, Theodore Roosevelt. Agencies were being created to administer and protect what were cumulatively called "natural resources." The universities responded with programs in the new fields, and Leopold became one of the first graduates of Yale's pioneer forestry school.

In 1909, this twenty-two year old arrived at the Albuquerque train station for a job with the newly formed U.S. Forest Service. The first director of the service and Leopold's philosophical opposite, Gifford Pinchot, wrote that "the fundamental principle of the whole conservation policy is that of use; to take every part of the land and its resources put to that use in which it will serve the most people."

As if in response, Leopold wrote, "A thing is right when it tends to preserve the integrity, stability and beauty of the biotic community. It is wrong when it tends otherwise."

It was this curious timber cruiser's perception and sensitivity that led him to conclude something was being irretrievably lost with the subjugation of the wilds. It was here, in what was then called the Apache National Forest, that he began to recognize the role of predators, guaranteeing the genetic strength and overall alertness of the prey species. An avid and lifelong hunter, he once believed that since lions, bears and wolves killed deer, their removal would mean game everywhere, a shooter's paradise! Some years later he would have an experience that would change him forever, recorded in indelible blood.

In the course of his work he had the opportunity to explore country barely mapped and often as wild as before the first white man laid eyes on it. It was a slightly overcast day, somehow charged with electricity; the energy of an inexplicable expectation raising the powers of observation and the hairs on the back of the neck. Riding horseback with an associate, they pulled slowly out of a quieting draw. They topped out on a narrow ridge overlooking a grassy bog a couple of hundred yards across. Reacting with the instincts of a subsistence hunter, Aldo matched the sudden movement below with the sliding of his rifle from its bullhide scabbard. He overcame the natural hesitation these familiar, dog-like shapes elicited, resolved in the time it took to shoulder his long arm and begin to draw down on these three blurry-grey creatures, running to escape.

The report of the first shot shattered the quiet with the disconcerting sound of an axe striking metal. A tuft of wet grass and mud flew into the air just behind the she-wolf and her yearling cubs, who then doubled their frantic pace. He jacked another round into the chamber, never interrupting the smooth swing of the barrel as it traced their rhythmic movement. A seasoned rifleman, he knew to increase the lead and fire into the space just ahead of the mother lobo.

Even before the roar of the second shot, he somehow knew it was a hit. He felt the world seem to stop, the way it always does at such times—that totally silent fraction of forever, in anticipation of the bullet's certain strike.

Her tumbling finally stopped, and they began to breathe again, visible as small drifting clouds in the crisp morning air. Except for the strange way she snapped and bit at her wound, she had died like any other animal. She bounced like the fleshy cottontail, slid to a stop like the tasty mule deer, kissed the earth like a fallen quail. Subsequent rounds sought out the scrambling pups, ending forever their wolfen dreams. They rode slowly to the site and dismounted onto the muddy ground.

"We reached the old wolf in time to watch a fierce green fire dying in her eyes. I realized then, and have known ever since, that there was something new to me in those eyes—something known only to her and to the mountain."

He knew that fire would be missed by the deer, the mountain, and that wild spirit howling back from inside himself.

"Harmony with land is like harmony with a friend; you cannot cherish his right hand and chop off his left . . . you cannot love game and hate predators. The land is one organism."

The precepts for which he would one day be known took root here, ready to blossom into a land ethic, and a legacy. He would write extensively on the vigorous balance of nature, describe the flux and power of wilderness for those who might otherwise never see it, eventually illustrating a set of selfless values for the Deep Ecologists of the generation to follow.

Aldo died in 1948, at the age of sixty-one. Until that time his works were largely unread outside of the university classes he'd spent the remainder of his life teaching. It wasn't until the 1960s, after publication of Rachel Carson's revolutionary *Silent Spring*, that his *Sand County Almanac* and its poignant essay, "Thinking Like a Mountain," became the cult classic it is—required reading now for most students in environmental studies, forestry or wildlife management, attesting to its current relevance.

In this period of worldwide environmental degradation, the fate of humanity is linked to the fate of nature. The question arises if we can ever have social equality without extending this justice to the many other life forms. By preserving the integrity of other species, we thereby preserve our own. Leopold calls for a progression in this Earth community from caretakership to *membership*.

Clearly it's those raw, upright mountains behind the bronze plaque that are the real monuments to Aldo. Some forty miles further north of "Leopold's Vista" the paved road forks. To the west lies Luna, a high-valley village named for the family he married into. To the right is Reserve, with its less than a thousand inhabitants, surrounded by three and a half million acres of public land. Like this highway, both the young Leopold and a sibling Forest Service came to a crossroads here.

Once ignored or summarily dismissed as "radical," his ideas have helped shape the attitude, methodology, and direction of those agencies legislated to protect our natural heritage. The Endangered Species Act, the wilderness areas following the Gila's lead into protected status, as well as state successes in the promotion of wildlife, owe much to the influence of Aldo Leopold.

Entering the difficult 21st century, we will be forced to reverse our alignment of priorities, inspired to improve upon our limited ethic. Witnessing human needs expand with the exploding population, watching the last wild places endangered by short-sighted goals, it is time to rush beyond the resource approach. Traveling down the asphalt arteries bisecting Leopold's "land of enchantment," I remember his asking us to rethink the meaning of "progress":

"Development is not a job of building roads into lovely country, but of building receptivity into the still unlovely human mind."

The Inferior

The animals we call inferior
see with their hearts,
live their lives in a harmonic fulfillment
we can only imagine.

Whether eating or being eaten,
they are at one with their world.
With our hate and greed,
our undeserved arrogance,
our confused and distracted minds,
it is we who are inferior.

We are at best only *equal*—
made worthy
through the determined strength
of our love.

To Put It Simply

Insanity is a piece of your mind
where there's no place vast enough
to get lost in.

Hell is a planet
under one unending roof.

Freedom is the option
to be yourself.

And wilderness—
the disappearing medium for freedom.

RUN LION RUN

I am stalked by fate, its padded steps persist in following me, matching me gait for gait. It's a sound so soft, almost no one hears fate's certain approach. They treat me like a madman, keeping their distance from one who listens so intently, eyes ablaze to the apparent silence that surrounds us. I go to the "lioness" for my power, staring out from under my furry brow, across the mountain peaks to the far lights of the city. I match the feline cries of fate, scream for scream, sounding dry and fragile in the chilled air.

We are the conscious participants in destiny's drama, called on to react. To act. To be the full-loving students of sensation and awareness. Differentiating the touch of every snowflake lightly landing on our hairless skin.

On this quest I've spent years getting personal with the wild traits of this country, the places too rugged for that kind of human I seek to avoid. I've learned some secrets from the raven and the coyote. I can approach within a very few yards of watchful deer. I can climb to seemingly unreachable eagle nests, surprise bristling peccary at the downwind entrance to their hideaway. The blue jays no longer let loose their raucous warning calls as I glide beneath their arbor.

I have seen almost every kind of creature that calls the wilderness its home, and I have shared with them vistas that are the birthplace of the winds. Yet there is one animal I have never seen. I have only heard them, lying there like our shared destiny, just barely beyond the frustrating limits of vision.

It was the kind of crystalline morning whose whiteness is all the whiter for its scarcity, here in Leopold's playground. I carefully followed the tracks of the solitary huntress, up through Brush Canyon past the scars Cooney left. I followed her through the ruins of the mining town they call Mogollon, its board shacks reabsorbed by the gnarly roots of cedar and piñon; its metal machinery rusting back into the Earth, filling seams emptied of gold with their flowing iron oxide. I used all the tricks in my bundle: the strategies I learned from brother peregrine and those rampant instincts I have inherited from the wolf clan. Twice in twelve hours I was so close that the edges of the tracks were still falling in, melted snow-puddles in the bottom from the touch of her warm pads. It was only then, at the sharp edge of nightfall, that I headed back down my trail to the wood-heated cabin below.

Then, suddenly, there on *top* of my tracks, were hers! It was stark evidence of where she had, in turn, followed me! It was more than the cool breeze of sunset that awakened every cell of my being, that sent shivers up my spine. It's not true what they say, that "you can't eat tracks." From her tracks I drank my fill of her estranged wildness, consumed her endangered passion, absorbed the precious significance of her rarity. I stood at the brink, spent in awe, floating, the way we float through the dream-ether of after-sex. Feeling both alive and fulfilled!

Run, Lion! Run! These mountain sides would not be the same without your sensual touch, your sacred touch. Run from the killers and the condos that spell your doom in dollar signs. Your every move is a perfected ballet, a complete poem one must deserve to see. The deer owe their strength and alertness to you. The wild turkey owe their pounding wings to you. Run, Lion! Run! You are the spirit that fills me.

It Seems So Obvious

It seems so obvious that
there'd be no species extinct,
no vanishing rainforest,
no statues of generals
with blood on their hands,
no lingering screams
of their cooperative victims,
if only the Earth came first.
There'd be no punk rockers
writing their names in the red of their wounds
on the parking lots of L.A.,
no angry-eyed police,
no courts stomping out
our individual rights,
or the rights of other lifeforms.
No homage to money,
loggers masturbating with chainsaws,
unbreathable air,
undrinkable water,
dams on our rivers
or acid in our rain,
if the Earth came first.
No asphalt choking out life,
infectious, viral cities,
cancerous swelling population.
No unwanted bambinos
in ashtray depots,

Goodwill boxes,
Austin, Hollywood, Denver
broken-glass alleyways.
No paeans to success,
no politicians,
no evangelists preaching damnation
and privileged access to the Spirit.
No hunger or foodstamps,
prejudice or indifference,
glitzy billboards full of lies,
or grimacing roadkills.
There'd be no maggot cattle
on wilting prairies,
no vanquished tribes,
hogans bulldozed,
ruins ransacked
for New York cocktail conversation pieces,
no questions unanswered,
yet nothing taken for granted,
if the Earth came first.
There'd be no unheard children,
suppressed wives,
insecure menfolk,
frantic, greedy bankers,
or abandoned elders,
if the Earth came first.
No fences in her fertile body,

oil wells
stabbing into her sides,
no picture tubes
to suck our brains out,
no lost and lonely artists' souls
unable to touch ground.
No musicians without listeners,
painters without lookers,
words without understanding.
There'd be no rock moved, without love,
no animal killed, without love,
no plant pulled, without love,
no one married, without love,
no one buried, without love,
if the Earth came first.
There'd be no fear of soil on your feet,
or little animals scurrying inside your walls.
No fear of the natural,
or fear of your dreams.
No fear of the dark,
or fear of the light.
No fear of death,
no fear of life . . .
if the Earth
came
first.

THE POETICS OF DEEP ECOLOGY

(For Gary Snyder)

When Bill Devall speaks of the arts as the cutting edge of Deep Ecology, I can feel it! It's like walking the edge of the sword, out there, away from your safe anonymity and the certainty of your seclusion. It is the responsibility to act that comes with awareness, painting the "tiger in the eye" that knocks off the viewer's comfortable blinders. It is the *myo,* the mystery behind the clouds, that entices the mind to expand, titillates its unused right side. It is the naked exposure of wildness that excites us to dream. The text and substance of Deep Ecology is more poetry than prose, describing a way of being and seeing that is deeper than the eyes. It is a sensitive and committed lifestyle filling the void with color as the arts cut away the bullshit. Reviewing our lives and arts from a higher standard, their greater intent.

Poems are images stripped of pretensions like a body unclothed. They are more effective this way, like a swimmer freed of encumbrances. They are at their best simplified as close to the root syllable, to the primitive grunt and sigh as possible without sacrificing the message. True poetry is set to rhythm not unlike a heartbeat, or the complex patterns of jungle drums. It is freed of the superfluous until, as perfect as a feather, as magical as a shaman's potion, it helps the reader to fly.

Gary Snyder writes, in *The Old Ways,* "One of the few modes of speech that gives us access to that yogic or shamanistic view is poetry or song . . . I like to think that the concern with the planet, with the integrity of the biosphere, is a long and deeply rooted concern of the poet for this reason: the role of the singer was to sing the voice of the corn, the voice of the Pleiades, the voice of bison, the voice of antelope. To contact in a very special way an 'other' that was not within the human sphere; something that could not be learned by continually consulting other teachers, but could only be learned by venturing outside the borders and going into your own wilderness, unconscious wilderness. Thus, poets were always 'pagans' . . ."

Good poetry is not cute and clever phrases stacked in deliberate array. Good poetry bursts out of the subconscious in spite of our restraints, in those rare electrified states. It is then that pure image, lessons stripped down to their cutting edge, arc through us from an essence *greater* than us. Where they touch the paper their passion burns their image indelibly, as if scorched by lightning. It is the perfect moment, lost forever if you look away, yet seeming to disappear if you stare. No deliberate manipulation can replace the perfect moment. It is temporal, and fragile in this way. Yet this is what gives it its power, its access to the source, the spirit.

Poems set out to stalk the mundane preconception that is suffocating our potential as a species and the entire sacred planet. Poems with a bounty on them, hung upside down on fence posts by irate ranchers of supposed civility; poems in the unemployment line and on the front lines of the battles; poems taken to court for extremism, poems loaded into the weapons of the oppressed.

Urban man's daughters hidden away from poem's honesty . . .

We earn power-dreams through our unselfish heroics, and through dreams we are inspired again to act. To draw the line. And to write words that take off, like the man Everett Ruess, showing us the way of no turning back.

MUSIC AND NATURE

The living planet is not only diverse, but polyrhythmic. Beginning at the most basic atomic and molecular levels, the elements of substance are held together not so much by the static laws of physics, as by the principles of music. Contemporary holistic science refers to "the dance of the atoms," a choreography that can be traced in the designs of wood grain and rock matrix, the similar patterns in the currents of the river, or fire. They interact with no regard to membranes or borders, in perfect orchestration. Every manifestation of the natural world remains unique in its song, and yet in-tune with the whole. In this way, intellectualizing humans, divorced from their source, join the products of their alienation (cities, plastics...), as "poor songs." Dissonant. Cacophonous. Out-of-tune. Hope for humanity is linked to hopes for the suffering planet. Our healing is recognized as a matter of tuning, the first step of which is to learn how to listen . . .

Listen! The energy of this living planet rings out as clear as a bell on a moonlit fall night. We experience its subtler emanations more through our bones than our eardrums. Our mineral skeleton acts as an antenna for these ageless cyclic rhythms. It rolls through the dry bottoms of the canyon country like a heavy, invisible wind. We put our heads down to the night-cooled bedrock the way we once set our youthful ears to the smooth rails, awaiting the tell-tale vibrations of approaching trains. We hear a flash flood pounding down from the high-country, unstoppable destiny, the thunderous flapping of giant granite wings . . .

It is the sound of the distant and heroic past rushing to meet the impending future. It is geologic time ringing through rock and strata, and the roar of the Earth's blood in our ears. It is the tangible, wordless lesson of the "old-ones," spirits of the animals and the first two-leggeds.

> "If you talk to the animals, they will talk with you, and you will know each other. If you do not talk to them you will not know them, and what you do not know you will fear. What one fears one destroys."
> — Chief Dan George

From the all-too-common tourist look-outs, the Grand Canyon appears distant and untouchable, a postcard panorama framed at the bottom of our sight with fencing designed to dampen our curiosity to see the bottom . . . or to fly. Each step down cuts not only through rock but through time itself, vermilion and crimson mirrors polished by the winds of change, reflecting ages long past. Across the giant canyon, barely out of sight, dust rises from the many uranium mines licensed to plunder and pollute just outside park boundaries, while somewhere far below the Rio Colorado patiently continues sculpting this wonder of the world.

Each layer deeper—strata under compounding pressure—rocks seem to hum tighter, vibrate faster. At the bottom the tension is ripe for resonance and, like the desert drum's taut head, waits to bounce sound high into the air. The countless colors are like individual notes, each hue a musical nuance, intertwining into a harmonic fabric that is at once both still and moving, alive! The canyon vibrates with a chromatic verve from out

of the past, and into an uncertain future.

The dance of the rocks is so tight, their molecules vibrating so fast, that they mistakenly seem solid. They wear the illusion of permanence like antique lace, appear unchanging through the shifting patterns. Since our tribal Pleistocene past we have sought it out, men and women of every color sculpting totems to last the ages, carving away the smoke-blackened surface of their cave-homes to expose a design highlighted by the lighter rock beneath. Rhythms of time, created as one line spiraling out, looking at a distance like concentric circles, announcing the sacred places of the American Southwest.

It's always just out of sight, carved in the pink and purple surfaces of volcanic mammoths, locked into the unhurried pace of the geologic show. You come to it the same way you finally trace it with the shaking tip of your finger—tentatively, spiraling sensuously down the narrows of ancient river canyons. Winding outward to enlightenment and Father Sky but simultaneously circling inward to Mother Earth and our own real selves! Marking, as well, the endless migrations of the two-legged storytellers.

It reminds us once again that we are all indigenous to this "Turtle Island." Looking back a few thousand years instead of a mere few hundred, stretching our limited concept of "home" from continent to planet, we take on the inherent responsibilities of being "native." We share in our common village-roots these things: an intense sense of "place," art and lifestyle celebrating the sacred, a deep understanding of the equality of all creation and reverence for a spirit of which we are a part, yet which is greater than our individual selves. It was recorded in rocks and interpreted through song by Viking soothsayers, Druidic bards, Aboriginal dreamers and Zen monks. It is the unified power that strikes technology down with a consuming rust, spinning sand in a display of revolutionary circles. Motive circles that map our spiraling journey inward, as much as our urgent reaching out. To this we add a lilting flute, the regularity of a tom-tom speaking across the canyon and the rising chants of human voice, in wonder.

Soothing and seductive, or loud and powerful, it is the function of music to wrest your attention from trivial intellectualization. Like a clap of thunder or a sexy purring in the ear, music must leave the omnipresent commentator of the mind speechless. Whether accomplished with aggression or seduction, it is only with the flow of alleged reality and preconception halted, with the canvas clean, that the muse can enter to do its dance, to teach its individual expression of passionate awakeness. As the composer Lucia Dlugoszewski writes, "Such music is not expressing man instead of nature, nor nature instead of man, but man identical to perfect nature, bringing us to our very best . . . real, alive, free."

Every race, every culture has this ancestry of consciousness in common, staring out of similar womb-caves, over tribal fires to the powerful and mysterious world beyond; their teacher.

Various pantheist religions with many faces, many names for Goddess or God, and yet each sharing the sacred view, the recognition of the spirit in the trees, rocks, and animals. Recognition of the illusion of mortality, the life in every element, each with a lesson and a rhythm, each with its own song. Rocks hum . . . a different vibration from each kind. Primal humans, too, each had their own song, like a medicine shield of musical notes, a spiritual self-portrait. There were also songs sung exclusively by the clan, those promoting tribal identity, and those performed in harmonic communion with all of creation. Songs set to the universal heartbeat, pounded out incessantly on skins stretched over hollowed wood: the womb again, the drum. The drum . . .

Spirituality is at the root of much of the music of the indigenous peoples of Africa, the Orient, and the Americas blossoming still at the hands of those we call Indians. The first two-leggeds on this island continent sang to

53

express emotions, to teach a way of being, to celebrate life and a oneness with the rest of nature. The ancients of the southwest, where I make my home, carved and painted on the cliff faces the many manifestations of Kokopelli, the horned-one. The burdens and gifts of the world in his hunched back, always playing his spirit-flute, in a constant state of sexual excitement symbolizing preparedness, love and fruition . . . Kokopelli continues to inspire, to jam, to dance.

Native American music creates the feeling of magic through sound, and the spaces between sounds. The effect is an accumulative sensuality, liberating the mind of the modern perceptual straightjacket, then building to a climax where the listener and the rest of the natural world blend. Amerindian music is an invitation to the mysterious, not to be resolved but reveled in. Their songs celebrate absolutely every aspect of existence, from birth songs, to those bravely composed pieces of existential verse one greets death with. In each is a sense of the cycles of nature, the cycles of rebirth. Like a bolt of lightning, like the growl of a wolf—this is music that puts you back in touch with your senses; that blows petty commentary from your mind and leaves you thrilled to be alive.

In contrast, a survey of "popular" music today is a tour through the mundane and meaningless, the stupefying. It is an aural paradigm categorizing the meaninglessness of contemporary urban life. Each form of music is distorted in the static and mechanical motion of industrial reality. Purists and sonic sorcerers (mostly on the small record labels) have avoided rock and roll's decline into decibels, the sob story of country western's computer clonings, or jazz's staccato bursts echoing the nearby jackhammers, and speeding cars' passage. In each genre, determined and often undiscovered artists continue to play, like deviant DNA, in the evolution of meaningful music. Real music remains an endangered species, an anomaly of the airwaves. Consider the example of so-called "country western."

Every year there is less country, and seemingly less country music. True country is subjective, personal, and makes no apologies. You are not likely to hear much of it on the country music award shows. You can find it in archaic albums that stick with you like old friends and muddy boots, leaving a trail of tales for those who listen. You won't hear much of it on the "country" radio stations, except on oldies night. You might listen to it in the dark recesses of small mountain town bars, songs usually sung by their creators, made of tears and sweat and laughter. These songs have smells, like saddle leather, freshly planted earth, and sawdust on the floor. The voices are at their best unpolished, shaped natural like a crystal. They are sometimes grit-edged with the honesty of real experience. Here are people of the earth in sharp contrast and often at odds with the refined and impersonal civilized world that seems to press on them from all sides. They meet it with cynicism, satire, and the superiority a wolf feels to the overfed dogs in town.

Emotive instruments wring out pain and ecstasy, runaway horses and gurgling rivers. Free of legato, country music progresses in spurts like a buckboard lurching forward. The movements are deliberate and without artificial refinement. Historically, country music owes much to the subjective and ultra-personal approach of spirituals and the blues, drawing rhythm from English and Continental country dance tunes. Inheriting the mantle of the bard, the rural troubadours whose songs describe the soul and trials of the land, country performers are the American conscience. The experiences of rural America are set in lyrics to music that finds strength in difficulties, laughter in paradox, for listeners who find more time for cynicism than pretense.

Country recordings grew out of the popularity of regional radio shows broadcast live at first in the 1920s and '30s, ranging from the rural fellowship of The Carter Family to ramblers and rounders like yodeling Jimmy Rogers. With the addition of the "singing cowboys" during the golden age of movies, country music became a top profit-maker and suffered the decline of quality and bastardization of style that seem to go with success. By the '50s, the style had already suffered from so much polish and glitz as to be shunned by country purists who instead ushered in a bluegrass and folk revival that peaked in the '60s (and remains a small but devoted market today). Such purists are preserving not only a form of music, but a set of values, and a way of life.

Country music, then, is common people reacting to the contradictions of the modern world, suffering the pains of the heart, taking solace and inspiration from the sights and sounds and values of rural America. The degeneration of country western parallels the decay of substance in most "popular" music, far from its folk roots.

The original (archaic) meaning of "folk" is tribe. Folk music defined the form and biorhythm of the tribe. Tribal identity was maintained, fostering the cohesion necessary for the hunter/gatherers' survival. Each song held a seed, shared only with the trust of the clan. It bore fruit as wisdom, courage, and allegiance to the tribe's sacred view. But even more important than clan bonding, song-seeds renewed the bond to their home reinforcing the biocentricism that allowed them to live vigorously yet harmoniously on their land, inspiring their allegiance to their region.

Folk songs of the traditional people of every race, and culture, rightfully tell the story of their relationship to their homeland, celebrate the character of the area and its inhabitants both human and non-human. *Involvement.*

As long as we lived most of our existence outdoors, we were a primary participant in the overall soundscape, in the watersong, in rocks in the sun, chirping like eggs, in the rustling games pine cones play on the forest floor. We somehow felt and were affected by the subsonic voice of her geologic presence, the drumming of her heart. Until we moved indoors, everything was *ambient*, musical, imbued with meaning.

Once inside, the music stops. The birds are no more, the river ceases to run. What we call ambient music is the soundtrack for our indoor endeavors. "Ambiance" (or ambience), derived from a French word, describes "the specific *environment* or distinct atmosphere" such music elicits. It is wordless, adagio, the milieu of receptivity moving slowly like a wide jungle river—time to see everything that passes, unhurried, without comment . . .

Such minstrelsy is an attempt to recreate the peaceful bliss of the placid skies between tempests, the eye of the storm and its pervading quiet. To color for you the contemplative drywash before the inevitable floods; to induce that vulnerable state of mind. That openness and intensity of experience humans deny themselves in order to bear the bombardment of unnerving stimulus.

Too often, the composer fails as a catalyst of perception, ministering to a kind of New Age Muzak, wrung out of the latest in phonic synthesizers.

The Greek pianist Sakis Papadimitriou writes, "Today, playing the flute, congas, piano, saxophone, become an ecological protest. Sound emerges from within the musical instruments, directly from their source. And you hold this source in your hands, in your lap, in your arms, around your neck. Vibrations warm you. The sound touches you. It is not coming at you from a different, distant and mechanical point. Synthesizers do not emit music. They are faulty. They do not vibrate. The sound takes a digital walk first and then jumps into the loudspeakers. This is the only way they come to linger in the air wearing their spacesuits. These sounds are ignorant of the earthly environment. They do not possess the elementary quality of surviving in nature."

The synthesized drum and bass have robbed most country music of its responsive intimacy and rural flavor, ripped the spontaneity and emotive heart from the breast of New Age jazz.

Ambient music, when it works, lays us naked and unpretentious on the riverside moss, opens our eyes wide with the glint of sunlight on the rolling waters, encourages the use of our six senses with its mood of relaxed expectation. It contributes not to the contentment of sleep, but the immediacy of the moment, experience without dialogue—like hushed alertness of predator or prey watching for movement in the tall grass. It must inspire (meaning literally "to breathe in"), the way deer pull into their being the indicative smells of their environs—the aromatic clues to their survival, to the pulsating world around them.

One of the finest ambient instruments is the flute, whether wood, clay, or bamboo, long recognized in primal culture as a voice of the Spirit.

The flautists breathe their very essence into the hollow recesses, air bent over an edge into a soft whistle, both gentle breeze and howling storm liberated in measure by nimble fingers over spaced openings. A tempest in a hollow bone. Alternately, you can hear a tape of the storm itself, torrential downpour and raucous thunder. Recordings of environmental sounds are ambiance taken to its most literal extreme. The fluctuating experience frozen in time on celluloid strips.

Piping bird and water sounds into your home or workplace aids that total right-brain takeover we so sorely need, yet must never replace our insistent and direct experience with the *real thing*. "Environmental music" does not take the place of "environment." Rather, it should be an incitement for us to get "out there," an inducement to *protect* that melodious wilderness.

Like a tattered Quinche poncho, ragged with holes in its detailed and cryptic design, the threads of the human species are rent asunder. Indeed, our *only* purpose, our *only* work, is to weave ourselves *back* into the fabric of life. Determined, rhythmic, melodic.

True interaction is no longer just a matter of reacting to the rest of creation, but of creation reacting in turn to us. Our ancestral mimicry put us in touch with the prey we survived on and the power animals we learned from. Certainly music and dance, and probably language as well, developed from our interspecies communication, and with it our integration into the harmonic totality.

It's humanity's extirpation from the rest of the living world that results directly in dogmatic political systems and religions crushing biodiversity, usurping our freedom, and precipitating our extinction.

In sonic interpenetration, musician and listener are constantly interchanging, mutually immersed. In interspecies communication, as pioneered by Jim Nollman, we are not trying to "decode" a language. Language is too easily a tool for reduction, standardization, and demystification. It allows for scientific comparisons, mutual sterility, limiting definitions, and manipulation. The last thing non-human species need is a linguistic formula, a means for us to direct them. Real communication is a two-way sharing of perception, not linear thought. In the realms of instinct, intuition, awareness, and sheer delight, we have far more to learn from them than they from us. We are not separable entities, but what Jim calls "a network of relationships bound together by communication." The two richest forms of communication are touch and music. We must not limit the other expressions of this Gaia composite to our incomplete and biased conceptions of them. To truly "know" them is to know more of ourselves. Joining them in song, we hear through their ears. This is direct hearing, direct perceiving without the distortion of our mental process. We literally "chime in" on an extent opus, a work ("play!"), ever-in-progress!

We define ourselves by echoing incoming

stimuli, reacting to our environment based on the feedback we get from our own signals. Like the dolphin's holophonic echolocation, we locate ourselves, our place, each other, and purpose. What ethnomusicologist Charlie Kiel calls "deep echology" is deeper, wider-ranged listening, tuning the skeletal antennae to receive the "bio-feedback" of harmonizing plantlife and sonorous mountains, the dense reverberations of the Earth's core. They're trying to tell us something!

Once again we look to music as a model. Any lasting change in the socio-political systems must be preceded by a change in how we perceive the world, how we "live" it. The maestro's baton doubles as the stick we use to stir the cauldrons of potential, and the magic wand with which we call forth a healed, enlivened planet-goddess. With it, we invite the play of evolution, and the grace and throb of nature's symphonic movement. Our every act should be written across space and time as if it were our very last song—our one final gesture . . .

RE-FORMING

"In this post-everything-that's-real decade (post-politics, post-feminism, post-consciousness) there is a correspondingly decadent compunction to look good. Spiritually, physically, culturally: pose pretty... Even us spiritual-feminists urge ourselves to image 'positively': smiling, wise, benevolent, graciously nonconfrontational ladies . . . Goddesses of therapy, rather than bitches of politics; goddesses of personal well-being rather than witches of Global change... In the midst of patriarchy's metallic noise and violent self-pollution, we consume tapes of our mother's last, lost waterfalls, forest winds, sweet silence... Earth can be made sick, beat-up, enslaved, can die: she has a right to defend herself. She is not obligated to be nice, negotiable, non-argumentative, non-threatening. She does not need to look good. She is Real."

— Barbara Mor
(From "The Morrigan,"
Woman of Power, #18)

Reclaiming our personal interconnection with Spirit, apart from dogmatic instruction and organized religion, is a crucial step in our reinhabitation and defense of the Earth organism. I put a lot of time into fending off polemic attacks on the concept of "sacredness," from pragmatic revolutionaries and "situationalists." I am equally concerned with spiritualist obfuscation and retreatism, commodified into psychic pablum under an umbrella banner, the "New Age." If, as Mahatma Gandhi wrote, effective spirituality and effective politics are inseparable, then it is their divorce that devalues these new philosophies.

The "New Age" is a marketable category of Cartesian spirituality. Although freed of restrictive rationalism and scientific reduction, it nonetheless embodies Cartesian rationale, the assumption that all factors, and literally all elements, can be flattened out on a single, measured plane. It holds that everything in existence can, and should, be predicted and controlled by this means. It's a model that posits a world made up of interlocking *mechanisms* separate from, and ruled by, the manipulative human mind. It justifies the pillaging of quartz crystals from scarred Arkansas hillsides, purported to amplify psychic energies in ways that induce positive global change with no other personal investment. Indeed, the spiritual impoverishment of the industrially-developed countries calls for a second look at the esoteric traditions of other cultures and earlier times. Freed of its ancient role serving the warring states of feudal Japan, Zen Buddhism offers genuine spiritual insights into the contemporary experience. Likewise, we benefit from the teachings of Taoism, Sufism, Wicca and Cabala, untainted by their historical associations or prior institutional misuse. Their most significant value lies not in their recent homogenizing, but their integration into the current context. The ethereal is made "real" by the deliberate acts of change and healing it inspires.

New Age thought is an amalgam of spiritual arcana and modernist psycho-therapy. We need not be held back, once again, by intermediaries and "professionals," our experiential knowledge of Spirit subordinated to a new priest-class: well-paid gurus, channelers, and therapists. The paradox of making spiritual pilgrims is rationalized away in "Abundance Workshops" reifying the material benefits of "green energy." We all must be compensated fairly for our individual work, but the focus needs to be on the higher purpose motivating us, not personal benefit.

The one technological innovation most representative of the "systems approach" is the computer. We borrow both programs and terminology from them, practitioners speaking of our "erasing the old tapes" in our minds, or "accessing" the inner universe (which represents self-colonization more than self-realization). The rational mind, as "programmer," seeks definitive blueprints of its vessel's mechanical functions.

The accepted definition of "therapy" is the treatment of disorder, excluding surgery. This obliviates the very real value of disorder in an oppressive monoculture, as well as precluding the necessary surgical excising of destructive systems in personal and political processes. The basis of the new therapies is the premise that superficial alterations in behavior or appearance represent a fundamental change in our experience of reality, and thereby reality itself. Therapeutics such as "creative visualization" promise an objective, physical reality that corresponds with our mental projections, with no assertive efforts on our part. In this progressive vocabulary, assertiveness is equated with aggression, and dismissed as "negative energy." We are to remain pretty, composed, positive, and passive.

Dualism, carried over from the sectarian religious traditions we draw from, continues to postulate a polar world of good and bad, now seen as the result of our approach to it. Such psychic determinism presumes that every hurtful or destructive situation is a manifestation of our negative psychic projections. The assignment of culpability to the onlooker exonerates the transgressors. This is comparable to the judicial process which inadvertently places much of the blame on victims of sex crimes, alleviating the rapists responsibility for the attack. Militarism and war, inequality and environmental destruction are the cumulative projections of the social body. Our only individual responsibility for these wrongs resides in our acquiescence, acceptance, or direct participation. We do not create the destructive forces by "focusing on the negative," as some therapists would have us believe. In the same way, though, ignoring the destruction will not make it go away.

A basic problem with New Age positivism is its spiritual ostrich act, burying one's head (awareness) in the sand (inside ourself). At the numerous therapeutic retreats, clients wrap their psyches up in down comforters, pad their falls-from-grace, reduce their focus to the predictable, the comfortable, the safe. Seated in "sense-a-round" easy chairs, they are "treated" with videos of rolling ocean waves and towering forests, the same beaches giving way to condominiums and pollution, the movie forest being clearcut just outside the perimeters of the retreat. A recording emanates from several points within the upholstered chair, a drone similar to the audible buzz of high-power lines, or the combined hum of a house full of electric appliances. It's designed to elicit those soporific brain waves associated with the pre-sleep phase, overlaid with an endless score of synthesized music. More than escapism, it is methodical "insulation-ism." It's a journey through interplanetary space (blissful emptiness!), rather than the crucial spiritual and mental introspection required to effectively impact the "external" world.

The diverse, esoteric music of personal exploration is alive and well, crammed together under the label "New Age." They are shelved next to the synthetic (artificial?), light (trivial?), relaxing (anesthetic?), easy-listening (undemanding?) genre I call "Space-Muzak." It is these recordings, of all the packaged accoutrements of "capital" spirituality, that best illustrate its weaknesses. The debility of both the style of music, and its philosophical parent, results not from their traits, but those traits they lack. They languor without fire, risk, serendipity, acoustic realism, suspense, variation, build-up or climax. Tonally, they are all shield and no sword. They lack the immediacy and vital tension that sustain form. The mindset, like the compositions, ask nothing of us. Muzak is the soundtrack of waiting rooms, and we have no time to wait.

The more vacuous recordings join the independently beneficial approaches of meditation, "affirmation," and other psychosomatic devices in *collective* disservice. These benign methodologies are dissipative, unless manifested in the physical and socio-political environments. Otherwise, they defuse our reactions to justifiable anxieties, deferring conflict to a safe distance or still-future time. They may engender a false sense of psychic security, allowing us to postpone dealing with the global emergency unfolding around us. Too often we shelter ourselves from feelings of powerlessness, emptiness, and entropy with insulating practices that do nothing to challenge the structures and assumptions that spawn these emasculating emotions in the first place.

The most personalized spiritual traditions deal instead with the uncloaking of our inner beings, the disregard of comfort and stripping away of protective insulation. These include primitive rites of passage, initiations, vision quests, the flesh-piercing Sun Dance of the American Plains tribes ... They relieve us of superficial costumes—vanity, pretense, ease, habit, certainty—and strip us down to the raw experience of inner-self, wild-self, soul . . .

It is the *intensification* of sensation, not its sublimation, that reconnects us to the spiritual flux, the *real* world. We can enter this reality only as a child would, deliberately, purposefully, assertively—and with humility, amazement and wide-eyed wonder!

The completeness-of-being all holistic practices address lies within each person. The redeeming effort is not to become it, but to *be* it. Rather than transform, we need to reform, in the original meaning of the word, to return-to-form. We experience not only our inner selves, but our greater, interconnected, planetary identity, a kind of "greater-self realization," in which we know ourselves as all-inclusive Gaia. We feel the righteous rage of the wounded goddess.

The Earth doesn't need a "man"-made program for the simple survival of humanity, or even the continued survival of other lifeforms. It needs the complete liberation all personal, social, and biological potentiality. The *integrity* of the complete biota is elemental to humans' fullest actualization.

The significant good in what is called for a time, "New Age," lies in its contribution of varied tools for our physical and spiritual healing. Mending. Making the rent edges touch. The reformation of lethal social and political paradigms will be the result of cataclysm, or preferably, our own delighted return-to-form; enlivened, activated, intent—positively insistent.

Lone Wolf Circles

HARMONY:

The Myth Of Peace, The Return To Balance

Peace: "Free of conflict or disturbance."

There is no peace in the natural world. The ocean we named Pacific is anything but tranquil. What appears as peaceful is the occasionally calm surface, concealing mighty currents underneath. Even this is a moving line between two elements, a porous membrane where different powers touch. Nature's diverse expressions are the result of determined individuation. Life's many shapes are formed by the tension between opposable forces.

Life exists by feeding on life, the aggressive act of predation. Scientists have proven what primitive people already knew, that even plants experience pain when killed. Vegetarianism seems peaceful because we fail to hear their screams.

Redtail hawks feast on scrambling cottontails, buck deer crash headlong into one another during rut, trout chase other fish well away from their spawning grounds, and squirrels defend their nests with vicious bites and a furious stamping of paws. Aggression provides a service for the natural world, earning for each species the food it eats, the certain passing down of the strongest genetic traits, the survival of their young, the inviolability of their niche, and the integrity of their life's unmanipulated dance.

Modern warfare is depersonalized aggression, institutionalized violence on a massive scale. Other than hunting for sustenance, aggression in the animal world seldom results in death. Wolf packs do not form alliances to drive their prey to extinction. Even among tribal peoples, alliances were limited to shared bioregions, and the greatest honor in a conflict was to shame the other warrior by touching him without killing him—"counting coup."

The fault for thousands of years of genocidal warfare lies directly with civilization itself. It objectified aggression and set it to serve an all-powerful abstract: government. The resource exploitation and division of labor that began with the rise of city-states rapidly grew into the industrial factories of today's war machine. The development of awesome new weaponry parallels the depersonalization of aggression and the devaluing of life. We have thermonuclear warheads, with the power to destroy every living thing on the planet many times over, poised to strike people we will never know well enough to find a reason to hurt. Civilization has debased our animus, robbed us of our true nature. It has made us fear without understanding, starve without hunger, lust without living, kill without anger.

"Peace" is a false ideal, promoted by warring states. "Peace" is the static resolution all wars are ostensibly fought for. We "fight for peace," those times of pacification between conflicts when control and aggression are internalized by the people, when bribery and coercion are substituted for raw force, and therefore when power over the individual is complete. "Peace" is the public relations child of the war machine.

We wage war on the Earth as we wage war on each other. Civilized Europeans "discovered" a continent already inhabited by millions of indigenous peoples and billions of non-human species. They proceeded to "pacify" the native populations in deadly earnest, "capture" the mountain peaks, "tame" the rivers, and "conquer" the "virgin" wilderness. The analogy of an environmental war zone is all-too real seen from the middle of a devastated Oregon clearcut, listening to the blast of high-explosives at yet another dam site, or witnessing the Forest Service's bombardment of Vietnam-vintage napalm on East Texas forests to "save" them from insects. Even our pastoral road system is a veritable Auschwitz to the community of life it entombs.

We domesticated the Earth, never realizing we *are* the Earth, and that we have in turn domesticated *ourselves*. We share the specialization, infantilism, and diminished alertness of the cows and sheep we down-bred. Prehistoric cattle were magnificent creatures with incredible eyesight and unbelievable sense of smell. Their progeny were the test early hunters pitted themselves against in solitary rites of passage. Like the African tribesman facing his fate in the eyes of a formidable lion, the primal European hunter could easily become the hunted, back-trailed and ambushed by the wary bovine. Not so, the opaque-eyed cows of today.

We have pawned our once acute senses, until it is almost too late to retrieve them. Like those animals we domesticated, we are dulled by our comforts, debilitated by our habits, disconnected from our bodies, disenchanted in the face of pathogenic rationale. Technology is the puppet of civilization, the iron in the chains that bind us, the tool of our voluntary enslavement, and the weapon of war.

Leaps in technology are usually a response to these wars, or to the threat of them—complex advances that enlist and entrap us even as they intimidate or annihilate our imagined enemies.

The destruction wrought by multi-ton nuclear warheads is so complete, and so general, that no individual would ever use one to defend him or herself. They are used, instead, to defend *concepts*. Governments. Ideas.

Modern war is based on alienation and abstraction, not anger. Soldiers are taught to feel no emotions as they "neutralize targets" (never recognized as the living bodies of people we had no personal contact with). Mass genocide is a product of our depersonalization, not our anger.

The way to put an end to institutionalized war is to eliminate institutions. If we were willing, we could divest ("dis-invest") in them—denying them validity. Acquiescence legitimizes those systems and processes ushering all life to the sheer brink of extinction.

Our honest anger is a necessary counterbalance to this ponderous machine of destruction. Being emotional is not "taking on the negative energy" of the enemy, for this is an enemy without feeling.

Anger is a balanced and crucial response to the cutting of the last old-growth forests, the obliteration of the wild wolf, or the installment of the newest missile system in the heartland of this continent. The "plowshares" defendants, imprisoned for beating on live warheads with simple hammers, were responsive counterweights. The hundreds of conscientious protesters arrested each year for trespassing at the Nevada Nuclear test site are counterweights. In the looming shadow of Armageddon, it is feeling nothing and doing nothing that is wrong.

Koyanasquaatsi: World out of balance.

War will end, not when we "establish peace," but when we return to life-in-balance, to an equilibrium not only between each other, but between us and all other elements of nature as well. In dance, this would be called choreography. In music, we call this balance of differing tones harmony.

Our acculturation removes us from the natural composition. We are superimposed, discordantly, over the receding musical tapestry. We are separated from the tonal symmetry, the congruity of contentious elements in perfect balance with one another. Our quest, then, is not only to find "peace"—those moments of quiet between notes—but also to guarantee harmony: human reproportionment within life's "movement." Our activated response is choice minstrelsy, a contribution to balance, a melodious resistance. We go from the score-keeping of war into the musical score, re-living our rhythmic purpose, reintegrating into the greater "arrangement" of undivided nature.

The opposite of passivity is activism, not violence. There is no time for pacification. We are needed now more than ever to orchestrate the madness our civilization has wrought. The maestro's baton doubles as a magic wand, insistently provoking a return to the balance of a harmonic whole.

So Alone Now

Where are you when I need you?
Looking for your light on the water,
holding myself ever-so-tightly,
with both arms.

You were my last connection to "humanity"—
so alone now—
can't identify with my species anymore,
but for you . . .

I call up a vast separateness around me,
invoke clouds to smother starlight,
dance in ever-tightening circles
inside myself,
howl your essence on naked winds.

I am surrounded with obsidian oceans
and moonless desert midnights,
black millennia charged
with the still uncombined elements
of first life.

Feel all this
the way we sense soil-polished crystal
in purest-darkest night,
through the unblinking eyes
in the gaping pores of our skin.

Spirits are called forth
against merciless reason,
here, at this crucial juncture
between the frightening evolution of the soul
and the chilling suicide of normalcy.

I'm set still more apart
by the imperative search
for more than all,
closer than touch . . .

I make my way precariously
around the far edge
of the motive hoop.
My dependably wild behavior goes unnoticed
like the eternal migrations
of the forever extinct
and the not yet born.

A great suppressed suffering
rises unbearably in my chest.
It escapes my throat in unfamiliar,
dinosauric sounds
echoing across the umbric translucence,
ringing off Apache-Teardrop waters
like the most elusive seabird's call.

You have only to slow down
to leave me—
I scream for you
with a warrior's closed mouth,
spiraling backwards in pain
to the arresting dawn,
yet plummeting forward in ecstasy,
through miraculous eternity once more.

EARTH EROS

The world is ever consuming itself, ever making love to itself through its constituent parts. Each element of life, each dancing cell is at once the pursuer and the pursued, gifting a tension and excitability lost on the adherents of certainty, sameness, and stasis.

We speak of "Mother Earth," source of all things, in contrast to the contemporary view of the planet as lifeless rock—as nothing more than raw material and the staging area for "human advancement." We know Mother Earth as an ancient crone and bestower of Wisdom, but also as a gleeful child, haughty adolescent, and lusting, fertile lover.

Sexuality is the dance of change, the palpable expression of the evolutionary drive. As with a spinning top, it is motion that imparts balance.

Wilderness is unprogrammed nature. It is alive with sexual flux. It is the ebb and tide of sensation, the fecundate matrix of this evolutionary fervor, the alchemy of transformation. Wild Earth is a planet deliberately and actively engaged in intercourse, the interpenetration of all its sacred parts.

The suppression of nature follows the suppression of the self, as each is "moved indoors" by the erection of walls around them.

The seeds of our alienation may have followed the first planting of seeds in the ground. By planting our food crops instead of harvesting them as they occur naturally, we appeared to "take control" of our environment. With this imagined proprietorship came the concept of private property and the wars it prompted. It led as well to the end of the hunting-gathering societies, perhaps the most egalitarian of all human social models. Their members enjoyed a ratio of leisure hours never since equaled.

The tending of crops mandated a sedentary existence. The result of this urbanism was the development of patriarchal hierarchies, surplus capital, and the exploitation of distant areas to support the growing city-states. With division of labor came class distinction and the torment it produced. By the time the Roman Empire was conquering the last tribal "barbarians," the process of separation and alienation was well advanced. Men only ventured into the wilds to prove their "virtu" (courage). Nature was only to be loved as it became humanized—manicured parks, fountains, orchards, or the military formations of vineyard grapevines. Walls, with or without roofs, became marks of civility. To be male had already come to mean macho, to be aggressive. This implied a willingness to do battle, while to give a woman sexual pleasure was considered servile and pitiful. Passion must be objectified and forceful, for to fall in love made a man a slave to the woman temptress. The soul was now unfed, with the repression of intimacy, and without the indulgence of love.

Civilization, through the decrees of government, religion and the cruelties of social peer pressure, labeled women and nature "dirty." Fertile soil and female menses were both equated with impurity. Women, like the wilderness, were tainted by their inability to escape their "base" functions. Fear of sex and mortality.

Bodies, once buried unprotected in shallow graves, enriching the earth they were placed in, were now secured in resistant boxes. Concomitantly, women were expected to engage in intercourse fully dressed. (The contemporary version has us making love only at night, under the cover of darkness and the polyester sheets of the dominant paradigm.) Women were expected to lie still and quiet, as any evidence of desire would be seen as craven immodesty and the mark of a harlot.

Wilderness came to represent the same threatening qualities for which later generations of women would be burned at the stake as witches—lust, power, sensuality, unpredictability, exhilaration, communion with animals or spirits, visionary enticement, and the free expression of wildness. Sexuality and wilderness represent the disordered and unruly, their fluids undammed, overcoming orderly human will. Both influence people, those necessary cogs of the new social systems, to explore the disobedient realm of the irrational, the experiential, the magic . . .

A lasting trend was established, masking sexually distinguishing odors with soaps and oils, while church and state defined "proper" sexual behavior. Today we have douches, vaginal suppositories, underarm deodorant, even disposable underwear without which we are convinced we will be offensive and never find the mate/career we deserve.

Genuine eroticism defies all this toxic pretense. It is also the antithesis of force, of institutionalized raped. Real sensuality calls for softness and sensitivity, an awakeness and giving that undermines the aggressiveness and competitiveness on which the techno-industrial patriarchy depends. To defend itself, society has legislated sexual behavior, channeled lust into conquest, and diffused sensuality with abstraction.

Examine our contemporary vocabulary. The term "to perform" sex gives us insight into the process of denaturing, reduced to an "act" under the strict control of our "civilized" will, a scripted "play." In this version of coitus, we are denigrated from participants to spectators of a "sport" we engage in. We witness the "act" from somewhere outside of ourselves.

Ours is a spectator culture, vicariously experiencing the real world from the bleachers, or through others, or through the ever present media. We seem to be watching the fire on the news, even as the conflagration engulfs our house around us. We insist on processing all input until what we hear is a mere commentary on what is happening to us. Our lives are taken up deciding whether or not to respond to the echoes of experience. This inclination to detach and sort enabled us to clinically choose which stimuli we allow to effect us, to strategically flee the potential pain of our subjectivity.

Passion, as I define it here, differs from lust in its adherence to subjective primalcy, to the personalized immediacy of the here and now. It is one of the most difficult of human emotions to fake. When passion is most real, it pulls us out of our shallow modes of experiencing, into the depths.

In the moment of peak experience, even the diehard escapists must return from their fantasy trips, thrust back into their body, into the present tense.

Passion is the worthy opponent of abstraction, of objectification. It is the ally of immediacy, of the unalienated, unsequestered, unrestrained whole. It is the flames you see with eyes closed. It is the melting point, the point of combustion, and as such, it seems to hurt. But it is the pain of our reunion, the pain of knowledge beyond thoughts, the sensation of being truly alive!

Under passion's influence, we are tossed about like a child at the beach, spilled by an unexpected wave, tumbling for what seems like forever, unsure which way to the surface.

Bliss is the outlaw child of passion. It follows this relinquishing of control. Bliss is submission, spinning ecstatically in a world-without-comment. It arrests the fragmentation of time, exposing a crystalline window on eternity and our own omnipresence. We ascend through the female energies. The path to the cosmos is through the Earth.

Sexuality releases that which we have suppressed, the female in each man, and the male in each woman. In passionate love-making, as in our fetal past, we exhibit the potentialities of both sexes.

Before puberty, we experience everything as sexual. Time unfolds like a blossom to be touched, an unfragmented continuum. For children, time is a tactile playground between dreamtime rehearsals. Life is at first a cave to explore, the revealing adventure of sensation, fingertip to fingertip with eternity, dancing naked in the eternal present-moment. Children don't "know enough" yet to close off, to imprison time in measured segments or restrict the animal joy born to us.

The child is then taught the "shame" of sensation, inculcated with guilt. We are taught not to touch even our own bodies. We dare not delight in our finger's travel through our own hair, touching ourselves only to clean and groom, or in the frantic, frightened paroxysms of solitary masturbation.

In this way, we fear touching our expanded, or "greater" selves as well, afraid of being soiled by the planet-body. We wear shoes that prevent us from making contact with the ground, "ungrounded." We cover it with concrete and plastic, wash our hands of its color. We run from the orgy of energies that is the living Earth, afraid to be unabashedly sucked into this passionate interplay.

The philosopher Alan Watts once corrected me, then a precocious adolescent ranting about "materialists" at his houseboat party. They are not truly "materialists," he assured me, as they do not delight in the material, in the texture and substance of life's diverse elements. They don't handle their food with joy, or pay attention to the way their clothing moves against their skin. We can see from this that those deemed "sexist" do not revel in their sexuality, dally over love's heated smells, or work to make love-making last. They never recognize life as a permanent state of foreplay, of arousal. They do not relish the spiritual and romantic plateaus their passionate desires could bridge for them. Instead, they resent their pestering drive, resent the opposite sex that "causes" it, and they grind it out like a butt in an ashtray in the briefest possible time.

Passion frees the societal adult, unleashes the child within. We return from that sterile sabatical in our rational minds, back into our glands, our expanding veins, the increased tempo of our breathing and our strenuously beating hearts. We join Pan and Kokopelli, the winged nymphs and the goddess, in a return to wildness.

Primal humanity acknowledged the sacredness of sex, and its use as a conduit of higher energies. The base and the sublime were one. Oral sex, especially reciprocal and simultaneous, held a special place in pantheist symbiology. It was seen as the corporal representation of the ethereal, the pounding flesh of the restless dream. It is where we are consumed, and yet only the ego, only the separateness dies. Orgasm was seen as the collapse of civility's walls, the dissolution of all borders. It is this sensual revelry that defies the reductionist order of modernist systems.

Unrepressed sexuality is therefore revolutionary. It is one of the purest expressions of animus, of intent—loving beyond words, reaching out so far we are in danger of falling forward. Beyond fear of falling, it is a place where love is stronger than pain or death.

True Eros requires Amor. The impersonal drive flowers with the addition of the personal. This includes the psychic as well as romantic connections, seizures of a personalized ideal. Eros loves Psyche.

And I love the Earth Mother through my lovers.

We are a slow-burning fire. We are flames like laughing children, sharing the nameless secrets, thrilling to the defiant pleasures of our animalness. Their breath lingers on my lips like dawn's wispy fog, as unhurried as our movements.

We access the cosmos through the Earth, the Earth through the womb, and the womb through this momentous, blissful touch. Our smells become one smell, charged ozone and thickened musk. Exploring every imaginable way to give pleasure delights me—makes me lighter. For what seems a lifetime, we share one skin. Minds spinning backwards, we are no longer individual, we are "us," then not just "us," but *all that is*. We blissfully expand until we know ourselves once again as the complete universe.

My favorite places to make love are outside, under the proud light of day or the spectral illumination of the moon. I especially like it in the moss-padded crotches of ancient trees and the flowering clover of some secluded meadow; on shaded grass during the heat of the day, or on baked sand as the sun slips slowly out of sight. Making love opens up my being to a world of amazing yet familiar miracles. Raw nature is where my nature feels best. I am moist as the dewy morning, emptied like a storm cloud, reabsorbed by my lover, and by the Earth.

At this special moment, the lovers become one serpent, grasping its tail in its open mouth: the completed circle. It is the muffled wilderness awakening, rising. Like stars popping out of a blackened sky, each element of our being raises its face to the oncoming wind.

We are released. We are everywhere that is. We are everything that can be!

The Way

The way
the rivers sensuously mouth
each glistening rock,
earth and water seek each other out
for sustenance.

But—
    No centralized agricultural morass.
    No master plan for tranquil valleys,
    dissected and cubed like "civilized man's"
    synthetic-fertilizer dreams.

Your soft strength fills me
like the always-flowing river
fills each and every crack
in its crystalline course.

And—
    The way trees send roots to embrace soil,
    while tossing leaves to the wind,
    you both hold me—
    and let me go.

Neither our moments or ideas
will be baited by jealousies and greed,
nor planted in the sterile rows
of those lumber-plantations of the mind.

No—
    Your storms break down my fields of cane,
    unleashing the seeds of new growth.
    Your tempests ravage who I am,
    leaving me naked, mindless, and aroused...

The way—

With Woman The Answer

With Woman The Answer—
Mother and lover.
Innocent yet wise.
Sexy yet virgin.

She would love me like the wind,
And without weighing me down
Touch every inch of skin.
Sleep with me without sleep.
Inspire me to be my best.
Moisten my dreams.
Tend my drum's beat.
Set my fur to dancing.

With Woman The Answer—

Child and grandmother.
Experienced yet naive.
Laughing yet quiet.

She would send feelings
Like wolf-packs
Howling down my darkest corridors,
Set nerve endings ablaze
In their passing.
I'd carry them like torches

To see in new ways.
Turning my subconscious out into the light.

With Woman The Answer—

I'd thrust my arms
Into her wet soil.
Become one—
                —with the all.

COMING CLOSER:

Intimate Outreach, Journey Home

Intimacy is the condition of personal, prolonged, and continuous contact, leading to an inner knowledge of the "other." It involves a purposeful *subjectifying* of experiential reality. It is this basis for the most intense *living* of our lives. It is understanding the world, not through word, or thought, or sight--but through *touch*. It is learning by *extension* rather than absorption. It is the way we thread ourselves into the grand tapestry, framed by a microcosm made of swaying blades of grass and mosaic pebbles, nose to nose, whisker to whisker . . .

Intimacy is a product of trust. We must trust that intimacy with another, with all of humanity or all of life, will not somehow dilute and devalue us. We fear what we see as the anonymity of "oneness," the point of ultimate intimacy when all borders dissolve, when the thin sheath enveloping us collapses like the walls of a sand castle, to the transformational touch of unity, to the moon-pulled tide.

Intimacy is a struggle in societies that teach mistrust. My dictionary reveals a secondary definition for "intimate." "Personal" and "closely associated" is followed by "illicit sexual relations." The dissolution of boundaries is so terrifying we brand intimacy as a perversion.

We bolster our sense of individuation with cultivated superiority. We pursue independence from our lovers and friends, magnify contrasts between peoples with abstract nationalism and religious demagoguery. The ultimate tool of our alienation may not be racism or sexism, but humanism. We believe ourselves somehow apart from, and better than, all other life forms. The dominant religions formalize a belief system that vests us with capricious dominion over nature in servitude. Secular dogma posits humanity at the apex of an evolutionary pyramid, an imagined superiority based solely on *Homo Separare's* mechanical ability to think, to objectify, to hypothesize! (from the Latin "parare," to arrange, plus "se," apart).

Separateness from inclusive creation. We postulate a reality in which the Earth is a lifeless spaceship carrying the raw materials for our clever exploitation. We dare to believe we can repair the disasters technology has spawned with still more technology, dare to believe that we are immune from the destructive processes our meddling has unleashed upon the world . . .

Separateness from each other. Urban psychotherapists recommend a "healthy distance" for "functional" couples. Detached careers. Unshared interests. Twin beds. Backs unrubbed. Obligatory and perfunctory sex . . .

Recognizing our tragic estrangement, the path of our healing, our re-membering is back the way we came. First, we reinhabit our "selves," our senses, feelings, intuition, instinct . . . using the "Adept's" tools for grounding and centering, including the disruption of segmented time, the abandonment of language, the disregarding of all habit and contrivance, and the seeking of visions (personal spiritual experience).

Tapping into our inner feral beings, we fan out like wolves in a herd of caribou. We reach out like roots seeking to join the intertwining patterns of a vivacious world, the touch that is *sustenance*. Re-experiencing our "selves," we can re-experience deepest, wildest contact with each other. Uninsulated. Unprotected. And undaunted.

In touch with our family, then with the extended family of humankind, and finally with the expansive family of all life. Reunification.

"Intimacy" comes from the Latin "intus," "within." It is a return journey that begins within the wild heart of each seeker. It dances within the embrace of our human contacts. It flourishes beyond all limits within the matrix of interspecies play. Intimacy massages that wild heart, extends that wildest soul . . .

We only truly "know" something when we enter it fully, experience through *its* modes of experiencing. And irrevocably, what we enter also penetrates *us*. It is this knowledge from "within" that is the gift of intimacy, the conscious touching of our emotional selves, of our sentient beings.

Draw closer now. Open up our circle to the spotted owl and Gila mulberry, the gray whale and the teacher of the South, the white-footed deermouse. Silence! Come closer. Nose to nose. Whisker to whisker.

THE LESSONS OF GAIA:

Earth-Based Spirituality And The Revolution In Education

Gaia: "Daughter of Chaos, primal goddess, mother of all things, the living Earth personified!"

Primary education teaches one form or another of consensus reality, programs a shared cultural perspective, instills a lifetime methodology of social mirroring. In this way, societies achieve the functional homogeneity their mechanistic systems require. Post-industrial humanity is by and large reduced to desensitized gears of the societal machine, dependent on the ever-more outlandish toys it produces for the titillative distraction that passes for fulfillment.

We are living an accelerated historical epoch. What we know to be a brief moment in geologic time, the pulse of a living Earth, is a momentous era of snowballing regimentation and both real and potential calamity. The rate of environmental destruction exceeds the dramatic devastation of the great Ice Ages. While an estimated hundreds of species of plants and animals vanish into extinction each day, the population of a single species—humankind—expands relentlessly past the limits of both social and biotic tolerance, under the imminent threat of nuclear holocaust.

The technocratic junkies run to the drawing boards of their government or corporate sponsors for a technological quick-fix, yet another industrial panacea from the same people and the same mindset that brought you the problems. Meanwhile, the often well-meaning adherents of a thousand hierarchial religions pray for deliverance from the reality their participation supports, under the strict guidelines of their dogma. Each form of retreat and withdrawal invites the process, the way protectively drawing oneself up into a ball exacerbates the momentum of a fall. Both "solutions" formalize belief, robbing it of its intimacy. They absolve us of individual responsibility, alleviate choice, free us from having to learn the often painful lessons of primacy and response. Too often we ask for kids to "reach out" rather than "look within" for the flux of truths.

There are no piecemeal solutions, and no stock answers for us to pass on to the coming generations. They face the demanding evolution of humanity or its unrecorded demise. Their preparation as participants in the alternatives must include:

1. Aiding their reinhabitation of their own bodies, recontacting their individuated senses, personal sensuality, and so-called "extrasensory" receptivity.

2. Aiding their recognition of their innate, primal selves, the instructive instincts socialization sublimates, the needs of the "real self" unimpaired by societal norms.

3. Drawing conclusions out of the children, rather than imposing them.

4. The abandonment of restrictive definitions, and the accent moved from "how" to "why" and "why not?"

5. Experiential approaches, learning by doing.

6. The value and practice of silence.

7. Rekindled play.

8. Taking them outdoors to learn from the natural teachers: the perseverance of the wind, the taste of the rain, the weight of snow and the danger of flood . . .

9. Refusing to reduce the amazing world to a predictable formula.

10. The experience of interconnectedness with each other and with all of life, a dynamic web that depends on the interaction of each and every thread.

11. The discovery of intuition as the conscience of the Earth (in total).

12. The unleashing of that source of all true "power," the catalytic force we call, for lack of a better word, "Spirit."

What I am asking for, and what I believe in my heart the Earth is asking of us is not school reform, but a complete and immediate revolution in education. ". . . not just the limited, half-brained learning which concentrates on reading and writing, thus making our children right-hemisphere non-literates," says deep ecologist Dolores La Chapelle, and not just a revision of teaching techniques, which avoids a necessary "revision" of the teacher's self.

Teaching in new ways requires thinking in new ways. Holistic education is a function of the relationship between the teacher and the student, therefore dependent on the way in which the instructor "lives the world." The curative lessons are those that heal the perceived schism between mind and body, inner and outer nature, humankind and the millions of other lifeforms, creator and created, self and spirit.

We owe them a chance to manifest their wild, primal beings—a chance at the unregulated immediacy, the intent, intense experiencing of life that is each moment miraculously unfolding around them. This primal awakeness was the world-view practice of our hunter-gatherer ancestors, actively engaged with a world they viewed as awesome, sacred, and a passionate extension of themselves. Primal children today, such as the remnant African Pygmies and Australian Aborigines, know the cycles, needs and effects of literally thousands of varieties of native plantlife by the age of six! More importantly, their knowledge of them includes a spiritual interaction between their life-force and the life-force of the plants on which they depend. This sacred dimension grants the intrinsic, inherent worth of every element of nature. It is the opposite of Judeo-Christian dominion, and is without the connotation of caretaker or shepherd over a world at our benign disposal. Bill Devall tells us that, in contrast, "the dominant paradigm in academia and most other institutions in contemporary (as distinguished from primal) societies is that humans are the center of the historical process and that *all meaning comes from humans.*" Radical deep ecology infuses the revolutionary imperative of the late twentieth century with spiritual heart.

I do not advocate teaching particular religions in school, but that we inspire in students a desire to explore that force that is greater than them, yet, that they are somehow a *part* of. This encouragement of children's *direct participation in spirit* is considered a "heresy" by the standards of established religion, "perverse" by the strict dictates of "school as preparation for work" pragmatism. Serving the needs of blind progress, growth and the moral status quo, the dominant educational system likewise disdains unkept wilderness, the petri-dish of evolution, the matrix of possibility. wilderness is a roofless "temple," a motive "church" and "classroom" that acts as an indispensable contact point with the source of their power and *purpose.*

Neither should we confuse this metamorphic world-view with "New Age" philosophy, which again asks us to "leave the body" and "transcend," rather than to "go deeper into yourself," "transmute" our creations, and "manifest" our vision. This is the crucial and paramount difference. Deep ecology recognizes that we cannot truly escape spirituality, because *we are it.* We cannot escape the environment, because we *are* the environment. Quoting poet Conrad Aiken:

"The landscape and the language are the same,
For we ourselves are landscape and land."

For the next few classes of first-graders to be sure of reaching adulthood, let alone of obtaining real, elemental and spiritual self-realization, will require that we prepare them as catalysts of change, co-enzymes of a planetary alchemy. Our support of their diversity is the only chance of a pluralistic and equitable "tribe." Our contribution to their creative deviation and personal empowerment may be the last opportunity for a metamorphic rather than cataclysmic "cleansing." It was prophesized, long before the Old Testament of the Christian Bible, in the Hopi prophecy, the Mayan predictions and even the saga of my Viking ancestors (Ragnarok) in which the earth opens up like the jaws of a giant wolf and the sun is darkened for a time, before shining again on a balanced planet.

Primal mind is spiritual mind, a consciousness that Jamake Highwater calls non-linear, "ageless, raceless, since it has been the means by which all eras and all races have articulated one of the grandest and most exceptional aspects of human possibility . . . the most linear and material minds are not aware that history has relentlessly moved past them, putting their values in a new perspective which they cannot see."

Our repressed primal minds and the surviving primal minds of children sense not only the excruciating beauty of existence but the building storm clouds of impending disaster. Rather than shield them from reality and their incisive intuition, help them avoid resignation and dejection through the free expression of joyous anger and celebration of being.

Rainforest activist John Seed puts on the invaluable "Council of All Beings" for children and adults alike, where he asks us to "Remember again and again the old cycles of partnership. Draw on them in this time of trouble. By your very nature and the journey you have made, there is in you deep knowledge of belonging. Draw on it now in this time of fear. You have earth-bred wisdom of your inter-existence with all that is. Take courage and power in it now, that we may help each other awaken in this time of peril." What better description of a teacher than a "vehicle of awakeness." Schools that prop up the destructive paradigm at all costs stand in the way of any education. They are the servants of this massive construct and the inevitable entropy it engenders.

Both modern anarchists and practitioners of home schooling (such as John Holt) suggest the complete dissolution of school as we know it. To do any less than totally liberate children from all forms of patriarchal manipulation and cultural preconception is to accept our very subjective desire to nourish a compatible value system. By accepting the responsibility for these fallible concepts of morality, we are called upon to end our pretense of objectivity, our arrogant certainty, left-brain dominance, and ninety-nine percent of what we *think* we know about education. The "real work," says poet Gary Snyder, is to "make the world as real as it is and find ourselves as real as we are within it."

Our only job then, is to supply youth with the pigments with which to color their dreams, the room to discover who they are and the inspiration that will aid them in knowing what to do with their special selves. We need to recognize the individual spark of each child's vision, and then step back and fan those flames. Encouragement, not control. Alternatives, not stock solutions. We help them access the variable perceptions of a divergent humanity and diverse, polyrhythmic nature. Holistic education is the creative process of relating to not only the "whole" child, unfragmented and free, but to the organic wholeness of a living Earth—the biota of liberation, the flesh of spirit.

From Bill Devall:

"We are dancing on the brink of our little world of which we know so little; we are dancing the dance of life, of death; dancing the moon up in celebration of dimly remembered connections with our ancestors; dancing to keep the cold and darkness of a nuclear winter from chilling our bones; dancing on the brink of ecological awareness; dancing for the sake of dancing without analyzing and rationalizing and articulating; without consciously probing for meaning but allowing meaning in being to emerge into our living space."

Education as dance.

"For us, it may be a Ghost Dance for all that is lost . . . Or it may be the dance of a new revelation of Being, of modesty and Earth wisdom on the turning point."

Behold the flight of the children
to the valley of the dawn.
They've shed their grayness
(problems, worries . . .)
like vacant dusty cocoons
to the side of the bristling road.

Off through a red crack of light,
dancing silhouettes
become the outline of promise.
Hear the hurried beatings
of their translucent wings,
carrying away the one we know.

They'll rest from the tiring winds,
and build great rock barriers
at the edge of wild fields.
Untended sweet corn, fragrant herbs,
hand-sewn dolls,
and the indomitable fruits of the Earth.

Young bodies will bend and sway,
intoxicated with living,
certain of uncertainty, unafraid,
in endless, wordless awe.

They'll build cave-like homes
out of the aspirations of birds,
the insides of sculpture;

shelter each other with the colors
of their gentle drifting wings.

Witness the unbuilding of the winter,
the unbuilding of the social norm.
Babies will flap their arms
and bring down the world we gave them.

When love returns as a virtue
and forgetfulness becomes an art,
behold the flight of the children:
sons of wind, daughters of the sun.

Artist's Hands

Artist's hands are a gift of the Mother.
They hinge Earth to Sky,
span doubt and encourage the winds
all in service to the Spirit.
They fill the space between rocks
at the entrance to the sacred cave,
make sure the Sipapu is clear of obstructions,
separate what we think is
from what we know could be.

Artist's hands need more touch
than you may dare to give.
They give more love
than you may dare to feel.

Artist's hands
are the smell of sex to the deaf person.
They part the thighs of our mind,
intimately handle our deepest secrets.
They pull the steaming guts
from the still-surging beast,
tenderly plant seeds of love
in hot, damp soil
as fertile as menses,
as opaque as history.

Their sudden motion explodes
our dull certainty,
rips us to shreds,

then seduces us to live.
Artist's hands rail against compromise,
assault their own tranquillity.
Severed from the body of culture,
they make sniffing sounds
in search of a mate.

Artist's hands drink inspiration
from the polished skulls
of their conquered fears.
They write truth
with the look of innocents.
They give guns to the Indians,
swords to women and children.
They thicken their colors
with pearly body fluids,
sperm spent like spawning salmon,
bleached and drying
on these fields of possibility—
blank, stretched canvas.

Remember—
there is no one worth remembering,
and nothing human of value
not washed in the sweat
of artist's hands.

Unseen, under carefully draped darkness,
they form-up ritual

like heavy-breathing sculpture.
Shameless, they give birth to revolution
under the painful glare
of Chilean stadium lights.

At gun-metal sunrise,
at the muzzle-end
of government/culture's
deliberate misunderstanding,
artist's hands bravely expose a natural,
miraculous world—
create each full moment anew!

THE MEASURE OF THE STRUGGLE

"What matter a few bee stings, brother Wolf, to enjoy the honey of life?"
—Jasper Carlton

I thought for a while to be lonely. To weigh the spirit of truth against contrivance, relationships lost, irrevocable decisions. Weighing the results and rewards, and my pulling my art out of the prostituting galleries to better devote myself to my message. To the Earth.

Will yours be a middle ground, a placation, a satisfaction that allows you to relax, then quit trying? The "best possible compromise"? Mine will most certainly be pain and ecstasy, alternately, insuring in either case my most vigorous response.

Many truths are painful. All are wordless, beyond semantics. They are deeper than the surface layer in which man intellectualizes, fitting everything he experiences into a conceptual box, into a digestible vocabulary. I walk to leave words behind. To tap the female energies of wind and water, washing them away. My certainty is a black walnut tossed into the river. I follow it with my eyes until, where the sun's glare blinds me, it becomes light. There went the lyrics, but I continue after the melody!

All day long I walked, touched, felt, smelled the diverse aromas of nature. Pushing sensitive artist's fingertips into the canyons and valleys of roots and treebark. These are the senses modern man would abandon. I absorb the magic he would deny, a fight for the wilderness he would destroy in his greed.

Touching a still-warm bobcat track is like touching the cat. I can sense the bonding. And, next to the tracks, rotting: purple grapes!

A vine clings precariously on a cliff edge.

Each vine bears fruit only every so many years, so that they blossom in rarified air. And then, their perfect round bodies turn to the sun only a short while before drying down to the seed, or being swallowed by the birds and animals who covet them. They are only really sweet for a couple days, right before falling to the ground. Such was my luck. I could scramble from one wet glistening rock face to the next, clinging like these vines, eating the very last and the very sweetest. The harder to get to, the bigger and better the grapes. On a sheer face was a prickly cholla cactus, and cradled in its toxic spines were the fattest, sweetest, rarest of grapes. It was only at the farthest extremes of my limits, my courage, my abilities, my strength—pricked by thorns seventy feet above the boulders below—that I was awarded the best! No other day of the year, no other situation would do right then.

I have other times strolled through the unchallenging rows in cultivated vineyards, lazily sampling this kind and that kind of easily accessible grape. Like social humans in their social world, I could—without being in any way brave, talented, special—gorge myself. Disinterested, I ramble off, leaving this baited simplicity behind. Searching out instead, the wild, diverse and challenging.

It is through our struggle for Mother Earth that we are made worthy of her, not by the weight of our successes. So, with the barest of handholds, loosened rocks plummeting below, I face the protective arms of the cactus, taste that special reward I must prove to deserve.

Through it all, thousand-year-old cliff art figures watch my personal triumph, my latest lesson, and my sliding descent . . .

At the bottom, I press my hand once again into the bobcat track. It is cooler now, but we still feel our sacred connection. Freed of thought, I see once again, that we are *never* alone.

Lone Wolf Circles 11-78

Feather Rose

If ever you close yourself off to your dreams,
I'll open you.
If your canyons are ever empty,
I'll send rivers singing down them.
If someday your horizons seem to darken,
I'll send my friends, the stars, to lighten them.
If you feel restless,
I'll invoke bird-winds for you to fly on.
I've made love to the Goddess Muse,
and when you hit that one perfect note
I will make sure she hears it.

When only one feather will do,
I, personally, will bring it to you.

DRAGON-FLIGHT

The mountain is more difficult than the valley, yet upon reaching the top, the flowers seem more colorful, more alive!

There roost my dragons! Their iron claws carry me in a vise-grip higher than ever. Well worth the pain. From such heights all creation is visible, to be celebrated, differences accented, personalities sung. I revile in the rise of my eyeless way of seeing, in my distance from the stifling grey below.

True satisfaction is not comfort. It is wrought with challenge and growth, variety and struggle. It is intimately-passionately-vigorously-fully experiencing life through every pore of the skin, through heart and lungs, leaving the bones trembling beneath expectant flesh.

If there were no dragons on the climb, I would create them, most beautiful of monsters, to test our courage, our ability to learn from our mistakes. To stretch our potential to the limits, and then beyond. Expanding, honing our senses, an extended progression: adventure!

Gypsy boy. Lone Wolf. Apache scout a long way between water holes, Viking in uncharted waters, listening, sniffing the air. Looking beyond the horizon. I know the pain of the flower longing to open, the spirit longing to be free. I know the pain of forests being cut, grasses screaming beneath the pavement. I feel the pain of species banished into extinction and of human potential bottled up in distraction.

The bells of the Gypsy wagon have always called to us. They are tinkling out of the darkness of human resignation and the unseen folds of the future.

As we get closer, their ringing is the sound of the unchained brook, of a tongue in our ears, a hawk's cry and the whistling of the wind on highest polished cliffs. We can do nothing else but follow, in this grip of Dragon-Flight!

The Visitor

I lie in ancient riverbeds,
dry, so that I might thirst.
Semen tracks on lava dust.

I am always a child.
I am always old.
Tree roots in four states
feed on my drama.

Taste weathered buckboards.
Taste horses sweating, pulling.
Taste my loudest warrior yell
as I fill the sky with wind!
As I pick the wagon's bones . . .

I first saw you tracing pictographs
with your feather touch.
You don't fear the red dirt
that clings like life
the way others do.

You thrust your hands into my chest,
grip my passion in your palms,
roll my stones on your tongue.
Our smell becomes one.

Come dawn I'll rise,
send mystery and love
after your disappearing steps,
disappearing tracks.

Always a child, I'll do somersaults,
scratch sex and magic on pink-baked cliffs.
Always old, I'll extend my arms,
my body, my very molecules—
outward, upwards,
until the sun encircled.

THE INSIDE AGITATOR

"Just worry about your own backyard," they tell me, piling discouragement up on me like a wet, heavy snow against my lodge door. It's a cold steel freight train running over me with its sequential carloads of loneliness, poverty, and their soot-covered misunderstanding.

This *is* my backyard, the "Great American West," from the Big Horns to the land of the Mescalero, from Baja to the Chiracauhuas, from those orca-laden waters off Vancouver Island to the oppressed flyways of the extirpated California condor. My backyard extends, like a well-muscled spine, down the Canadian Rockies through the Gila, the Sierra Madres, and the enchanted Mountains of the Mayans. But wait! A leg stretches down the sacred Andes, dips a toe into the icy waters of the Antarctic!

Yes, but I also know some of the secrets of the Everglades and, like a ghost, I prowl the clear-cut eastern old-growth and those vanished southern hardwoods.

And more than that! My backyard girdles the Earth at the equator like a hug made up of the warm, damp rainforests of Australia and Guatemala, the Caribbean and Malaysia. It's all my backyard, cut up and sold, spit on and littered, fenced and drilled, entombed in asphalt until only the most astute can hear her plaintive cries for help.

They're wrong! I'm not an "outside agitator." I'm an *inside* agitator, working on the inside of this mechanical beast, this cancer. Fighting it bare-chested, exposed. Out creations and our actions are a loving balm that heals. They are also stone-chipped knives with which we carve at the machine's heart, defiantly cut our way out into the light of the great outdoors—the Mesozoic glow of the future primeval.

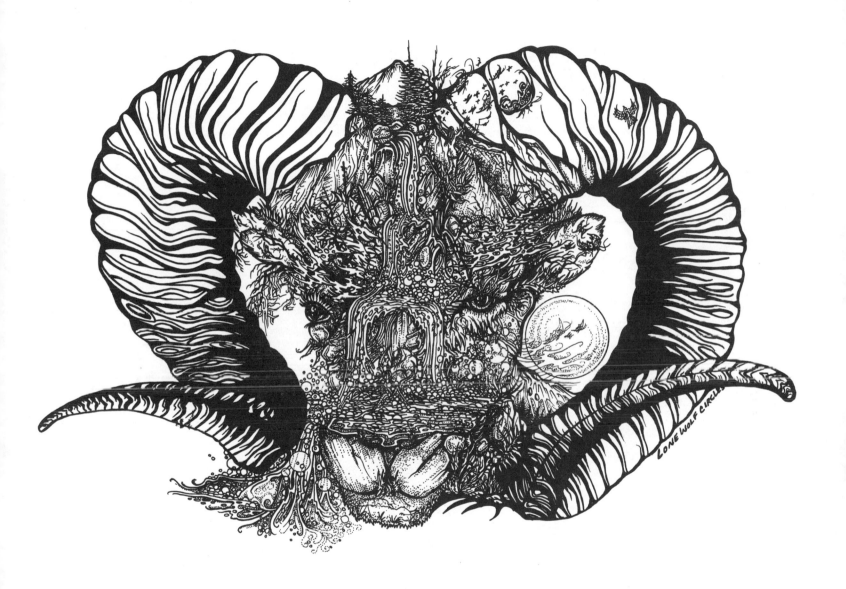

THE EMERALD CRYSTAL

The mists of dawn reflect first light like the naked flesh of mystery. We proceed quietly, here, where the giants grow. A pliant Earth caresses each reverent step on furry olive loam. Everything looks jade under the slow advance of night. Even the rocks are green, as moss and lichen padded as the ancient Douglas firs towering above us. More than a hundred feet tall, they encircle the fertile meadow like a solemn council of Druids. More than a miracle—their ancient cellular memory linking past and future in their gnarly patterns.

From the center of this clearing everything appears green, as if we were gazing out from the heart of a perfect emerald crystal. It's here we find that primeval calm, that uterine atmosphere that gives birth to inspiration, that pregnant silence from which depths we plumb our true selves. This is the quiet they would rip through with their incontinent power saws. Salacious machines, quivering beer-bellies—myopic two-leggeds who traded sensuality for unquenched lust, sentiment for increased profit, unpredictible dreams for a predictable role in a nightmare.

All wildlife retreats from the mechanical madness, those that survive our stewardship escaping on the blood-flow from the gaping wound in the body of silence. There is a flash of disappearing hoof and fur. Insects abandon their position on the undersides of leaves, and above us there's a frantic flap of wings—blue jays, owls, and robins with no place left to land.

Even the largest of the trees are killed; felled for dollars, felled for condos in Japan, felled for the paper which wipes our collective ass. The ridges raped. The mountains debauched. The rivers defiled. Every sacred place violated by humankind's iniquitous greed—until the sun sets on our dubious future, until the greens turn back to greys. Darkness brings a lull in the destructive clamor we call "progress."

This is the hour for the ghosts of vanquished buffalo and vanished wolves to take turns sniffing the tortured trunks, sniffing the blood that drips down the stumps to the oily sawdust at their base. Like whales beached by our "best of intentions," the great fallen giants continue to breathe. They slowly inhale the returning peace of nightfall. They slowly exhale a sigh, exhale a cry, exhale an urgent plea—for the life of the Earth!

A cry for the return of those reflective mists of dawn, in that hallowed place beyond the farthest reaches of the road, and beyond the reach of our sterile certainty. Exercise your mind! Feel your bared toes sink into the humus, feel them spread out into branching, exploratory roots until you can feel the heat of the Mother Source on the sensitive soles of your feet. Feel your body stretching ever upwards, your limbs extending to the sun itself. Feel, on the very tips of your fingers, the teasing, laughing motion of a thousand wind-blown leaves. Become family with the trees, and then protect them the way you would your family. *Become* the trees, and then defend them as you should defend yourself!

Another night has passed, and not in vain. . . It is here, in the first translucent rays of dawn, that we can find our place in nature, that we can see the clearest. This is the sacred place where we make our stand with the trees. Here, in the heart of the Emerald Crystal, where everything seems green . . .

Green—and growing.

THE RAINFOREST WITHIN

(For John Seed And The Rainforest Information Centre)

"The rainforests are the womb of life, home to half of the world's ten million species of plants and animals. They are presently destroyed at the rate of hundreds of acres per minute, and at the present rate, they will be annihilated within our lifetimes."

—Rainforest Information Centre

If only I could make prayer to the deities, my ancestors, the hunter-gatherers; to the spirits I've come to recognize in the trees and the rocks, to the Goddess herself. If only I could crack open the sacrificed mammal bones and decipher the secrets encoded in their spiraling matrix. If I could somehow climb the highest peak, sit silent the longest, interpret the pleas as well as the celebrations of the jeweled birds, somehow prove myself truly worthy to make requests of this magnificent planet spirit that creates us all . . .

I would wish, without speaking, that the greedy-scrambling-lost-lonely-desperate and distracted masses could for once become really in touch with themselves, with their real animal-aware selves. Re-enter their bodies and sense with all their atrophied senses. I'd learn that special music that breeds those steamy rainforest clouds, pregnant with that precious and pure biological basis all life shares in common. I'd send these powerful cloud-songs like inspiration, condensing into droplets taking wing on the winds. Thunder that sends cracks through their protective plastic covering. Entering through these, the droplets begin dripping in, like incantations, like invitations. They fall on flying scarlet parrots; like skilled-fingers on tribal drums, playing rhythms on the sun-touched canopy. Dripping down, form one oddly shaped leaf to the next, sliding down the sides of aboreal reptiles and twisting vines to where the roots of idiosperms drink up history from the source. Drips of awareness, finally touching humanity's heart.

Yes, having once discovered this rainforest in themselves, this awesome potential lit with new-found awareness, colored and scented with genetic and environmental interplay, alive with leafy-furry-scaly-feathered diversity, in touch at last with their own primordial and spiritual roots; an inextricable part of the world, no longer separate... Finding this rainforest within they would finally understand that the best reason for going beyond rhetoric into the responsive arena of direct personal action is not for any resource it might contain for us. Not even for its dynamic, wondrous value as living chapels for our children's children to discover their place in the natural order. Not even for us to experience its mystical solitude, living freedom, and unextinguished magic...

Let me tell you! Finding the rainforest in themselves, they'd know without a doubt that we must fight for these remaining wild lands and wild species if no human use is ever made of them, if no human eye ever gets to behold their special beauty. We must fight because they *belong* here, because they have above all else a right to be here! For their own sake, not for ours.

And because... humankind cannot exploit-cage-clearcut the wildlands, without simultaneously crushing the diversity, spirit, and wild potential within ourselves!

Tierra Primera!

WILDERNESS AS REALITY

Wilderness *is* reality! Compared to the breathtaking wonderment of the unchained wilds, everything else is platitude; fuzzy, vicarious echoes of lost meanings and forgotten experiences.

It's the difference between the sparkle in the eyes of a baby, unencumbered by the past or the future, responsive to all that surrounds them, and the vacant, tired eyes of an aging actor, forever lost in the scripts he never wrote, never really lived.

Wilderness is more than virgin meadows and pure streams, although it is the epitome of wholesomeness. It is the fundamental combination of land and space, whether harshest desert or unclimbable mountain, which in spite of everything has maintained the vital capacity of wildness. The wilds, like a splash of cold creek water or the unmistakable grunt of a sow bear, have the ability to rush you out of dialogue and into your senses. To stimulate your heart and get your blood to flowing like the powerful rivers coursing towards sea. Like sudden fear, joy or surprise, like a narrow escape from death or like root-animal lust, the wilds can so completely fill you with awakeness and a love of life as to leave no room for anything less!

Wilderness is a necessity not a luxury, if for no other reason. Humans, having abandoned the wilds of nature and the wild in themselves, replaced root-experience with distraction and abstraction. They argue over the details of environmental issues the way they discuss the relative merits of space movies and polyester fashions, football games and facelifts. As if anything in the whole world could mean more than the world itself!

Wilderness is reality, because nothing is as

real as the wild. Nothing as vividly experienced in every sector of one's being. Nothing. It reunites us with the pleasures of our hearing, our sight, our soul.

Take me out of these walls of habit, traps of distraction and padded comfort. Precious life is too short. Take me from the cities where money and the gadgetry it buys are the godhead we humble ourselves before. Take me from the walls and limitations I built myself. Take me to the edge of the crest, long past the lines of the aluminum beer can-motorhomes, above the static air of "progress," to where the winds meet in a display of impassioned power. Then take this rag from my eyes, and let me soak up in wonderment the beauty that costs only the heart.

Wow! Let amazement always fill my pores and ruffle my feathers, like an eagle preparing for an updraft. Then, all desires vanished in the completeness of the moment, I can be my original self once again.

Poet's Words

Poet makes words like howls,
against which curtains are drawn.
His words wander darkened alleys,
loudly kick at empty wine bottles,
reminding humans of their origins
by shittin' on the fire escapes,
making obscene noises
outside their windows.

His words play bass
for a blues band in Soweto
(unrecognized in sunglasses,
which, like the music,
do their work inside you).

In a Paris nunnery,
they disguise themselves
as folded sheets,
contributing to the restless dreams,
the uncertainty and lust
suppressed in the day.
Don't run—
Go to touch them
and they will rise against your fingers.

A few words are remembered:
A bit of fur lying on the pillow,
the mark of a wet nose
on their sliding glass doors,
the echo of alleyway glass
to an obscure "E" progression.

All continents are the same
as Poet bows to some modern cancer,
mouth open in the dust of derision,
still trying to articulate.

Poet's words press flat against the ground
as they lift him into the ambulance,
raise their legs in unison
to ceremonially pee on its tires.

Poet's words are like howls,
which, even when unheard,
continue wandering the foothills
of what could be—
Echo down the streets and canyons
of the planet-mind.

THE FIRST SNOW OF WINTER

Most often it arrives at night, waking us not with a racket, but with the palpable absence of sound. It settles on us like a soft blanket, quieting our world. We rise to wipe the steam from the windows to behold an enchanted scene, to be filled with its whiteness: snow!

Falling slowly but steadily, the giant flakes do their whimsical dance to a tune of freshness, touching down like a white satin glove held to our mouths, bidding us silence. Snow! Every branch is rounded, every line smoothed, every contrast blended to the whiteness of unspoilt art paper. Its cleaned canvas awaits the brush of color morning's snowmelt brings.

Moonlight on snow is something special. It transforms the everyday into the unusual. The familiar becomes the exotic. The trails we've hiked so often—even in our own yards—are suddenly strange and magical, the stage set for our child-hood fantasies. It calls on us to come out, out-of-doors, and explore this world of sensation.

There is something electric about moonlight running across the top of the ice like sheet-light-ning on water. It charges us with excitement, in-cites us to run and leap into the air, entices our earliest memories to come out and play.

Tiny rodents scamper beneath the shadow of an owl. Ponderosa pine branches bend to the ground, while the last of the cottonwood leaves drop with the weight of frozen water.

The snow is a hard teacher. It puts to sleep the green plant life, slows the bear's heartbeat, and tests the strength and determination of the deer. The same ivory casting that quiets our steps, records them. Everywhere are the tracks of animals we seldom see—the javelina, mountain lion, large-footed turkey, and our own tracks winding behind us like an echo of passage.

The first storms point out the icy air leaks around our window frames and the firewood pile that seems suddenly small and insufficient. The last yams and root vegetables are in the cellar or pantry now. Home-canned preserves line the shelves in anticipation of winter's morning biscuits.

Saddling the horses in the cold, I feel the cuts and bruises my hands suffered during two summers of work. The icy cinch on the panniers resists bending through the buckle, until at last I have it. Caught up for a moment in self-pity, lost in frantic waves of thought, my eyes are drawn to the falling flakes. Each crystal appears alike, and yet seen up close, we find that no two are the same. They each float in their own way, tracing a great artistic form, a determined ballet on the way to a destiny with the Earth.

Differences. Diversity. Challenge. Beauty. Together, the crystals form a slowly moving river on a journey to the sea. I breathe warmth on my hands and slip the gloves back on for the walk home. No regrets.

The old-timers of Gila Country knew the real meaning of "enlightenment"—a plow retired in ice, and the glint of New Mexico sunlight on winter's first snow.

Snow's Groom

Being the son of the hidden wild things,
I was the one chosen.

Unexpected,
the snow blew in like sleep
against a wintery pale.

All things hush
at this mellowing tune
of falling crystal,
a lively dance that blends.

The fasting wolf,
teeth bared to an ally wind,
gumming its essence,
then biting its freezing fate.

Watch: fur hood blown back,
my face hardens into illusions of warmth,
the ashen color of firepit rock.
Gone like smoke,
the paltry whims of my species.
I am snow's promised groom,
inheritor of children's crystalline delight.

Fertile frozen water,
carrying the secrets,
secrets that give birth to life
at the consummate quench of seed.

Stiff and giving,
I fall to the side
of the ice filled trail.

Impregnated snow covers my body,
like the forgetfulness of age,
and my gift follows the path
of cellular memory
(mountain goats, varieties of grass . . .)
into the spring river flow.

METAMORPHOSE:

The Deep Ecology Of Dying

Spirit is the highest fluid form of energy. It permeates, empowers, sets to motion every expression of life and so-called non-life making up the planet-body Gaia. It is primary to all manifestations, existing on a borderless and endless plane.

Energy is forever in metamorphosis. It cannot be destroyed, only transformed. Our identity may sometimes seem confined within our brain, in turn housed in a body that will all too soon atrophy and die, but the expanded consciousness of any true spiritual experience will show otherwise. Witness the unbound nature of our spirit! Death only appears as a curtain until you look beyond it.

It was the first conceptualization of boundaries that precipitated humankind's disenfranchisement from the matrix of the living Earth.

The "fall from Paradise" is attributed to the consumption of "forbidden fruit," rather than forbiddance. Primary alienation from our natural state, "paradise," began with our imagining we were somehow disconnected from the fruit. The rapidly developing left-brain function permitted a feigned objectivity, a remarkable distancing from the rest of creation no species had ever felt before.

It is this "original detachment" that cast us into conceptual Hell, full of false dualities between mind and body, humanity and an "animal kingdom," male and female, spiritual and material, life and "lifeless matter" . . . The development of song, myth, dance and ritual arises from an intuitive, right-brain need to maintain personal and experiential contact with the greater flow, with contiguous spirit, with the rest of the planet-body.

Our fear of death, and consequently our fear of the risks entailed in *really* living, begins with this illusion of separateness. All class and political divisions, along with the strife they engender, begin here. By imagining we were separate from the apple, we could then believe ourselves its cultivator, the warden of its trees, the evidence of its value, the sole purpose for its existence. By imagining ourselves unconnected to other people or cultural groups, we can then believe ourselves superior, believe that they somehow exist to serve us, that we are justified in fighting the bloodiest of wars to maintain control of them. It all began with our personal denaturing, that abject period of human evolution when our consciousness bailed out of our animal bodies, retreated in cerebral shuttlecraft into the "commentator" persona of our individualized egos.

Our narrow self (mental self) is estranged from the corporeal, divorced from its immediate body as well as the greater planet-body. Our physical selves are suspect, viewed as undependable instruments, fallible vehicles with too few replacement parts, briefly demonstrating a beauty we spend thousands trying to maintain. Thus, we are uncomfortable with the bodily processes that remind us of our physical mortality. We recoil from those changes that record our aging, refuse to accept transformation out of an irreconcilable fear of the "nothingness" we imagine waits for us.

Dogmatic religions serve up a cut and dried picture of the alternatives for an "afterlife," and simplistic programs for attaining the desired "reward." Adherents are taught about the visionary experiences of their religions's anointed prophets, while abjuring the grueling trauma of personal revelation. We let historical figures risk the intensity of wilderness and the pain of visions for us, while we continue the civilizing process of detachment, insulation, and escape.

Visions still stalk us, but we may not discover we are at the precipice until our thinning arms no longer hold, and our quaking thighs threaten to unseat us. There, perched above the abyss, destiny awaits us. It rushes forward like road signs toward an accelerating vehicle, passing so quick now we can no longer read them. What once appeared in clearest focus will be blurred in the speed of passage. We may find we ran the course of our lives without truly living.

In the seconds before death, one must finally experience that which adepts suffer from childhood and shamans come to know—the urgency and immediacy, the dramatic *precariousness* of our lives. This pervasive sense of treading "on the brink" is what fuels the rare flights of mortal humanity.

This flight is enlightenment. It is the awareness (feeling, not thought) of our universality, our psychic osmosis and the transmigration of our shared spirit. It means to be "filled with light," and then travel on its rays. One does not *become* enlightened, but acts it out. It remains a transient experience for civilized humankind, coming and going. One job of the curandera, of the mage, is to encourage this state of transcendent consciousness through whatever means, until it is indiscernible from "everyday" reality. Enlightenment is the dramatic return to the "whole" we abdicated—a journey inward not out, a re-membering (reconnecting) that heals the fragmented self. It is the return to balance, which ultimately requires the jettisoning of ballast rather than its clever repositioning.

Re-entering our bodies, we re-member our greater, inclusive self. We welcome a return to "ourselves," to the Earth in its totality, unencumbered by lead-lined boxes or hardened fears. We are happy to feed the worms and beetles, nourish the inquisitive roots of the trees. Consumed by the ravens, we too fly!

Liberation is the acceptance of our bodies, our planet-body, and the metamorphosis of our ally: death. It is recognition of life as spirit, in the perpetual process *of becoming itself*. The paths to enlightenment begin in a return loop through our bodies, through our inner being. The exploration of the cosmos starts with the reconciliation of our physical selves.

If, as the Plains tribes said, "it is a good day to die," then it must be, conversely, a really good day to live! A good day to sink our souls up to the hilt in the primacy of experience. Half of the Earth is in darkness at any given time, while half is forever turning its face to the sun.

The colors penetrate as never before. Imbued forms of the volatile moment sear the heart. Clouds bring tears, while the wind whips the moisture from your anxious eyes. Everything seems so palatable and potent, so significant and conclusive—so inescapably *present*, right here, right now!

I Call The One

I carry my loneliness in front of me
like a lantern.
Rendered alert with artist's anguish
and the uncommon demands of ecstasy.
I see well beyond that which I know.

Touch this thought,
smooth like the long sides
of a dolphin,
then tell me you can forget
I still call to you
from the outskirts, from the beyond,
as the other worlds on this one
call to me.

I call the one who can lift loneliness
from my hardened grasp
without dimming the light
that solitude has kindled.
In turn, I will teach you the whales' songs,
that you might share in being their guardian.

THE HEALING WOMAN

Walking attentively down the canyon, I suddenly spot the enemy, so obvious and so much bigger than us! I control my breath, ready my sling, bend over to pick up the only suitable stone in sight. I briefly feel its aerodynamic roundness in the palm of my hand before—

Fragmentation! Breaking up along a hundred unseen fissures, it crumbles in my grasp, escapes in a shower between my fingers.

Fragmentation. Too often we learn the concepts and perfect the vocabulary of a "subject," like "environmentalism" or "spirituality," without that visceral absorption, that complete and necessary osmosis. Wisdom is not something you learn, it is something you become.

Fragmentation. Millions stay mindlessly at home, hundreds show up for an apartheid rally, but only a handful protest for the environment. Right wing depredations in Central America, the arms race, sexism, social inequality—symptoms assailed on every lip-hip college bulletin board, while the common, root malady they share goes untreated. Believe this: there will be no social human problems without a livable environment. The same deliberate, patriarchal paradigm that oppresses nature insures the subjugation of humanity. The same world-view that justifies the extinction of thousands of other species each and every year will witness its own self-destruction. If we only battle the projecting symptoms and not the mindset that created them there "will be hope," as Kafka said, "but not for us."

There's no fragmentation in the cure. The social model that best suits the real needs of human evolution, health and diversity benefits the Earth as a whole: greatly reduced populations of culturally independent, matrifocal tribes. The "Healing Woman," the clan's sage, grounds lofty left-brain aspirations in the moist soils of reverence, aligns human wants with the needs of all life. She infuses ritual with heart, silence with meaning—an intimate conveyance of inspiration and wisdom, patience and respect. Familial gifts passed on from womb to womb, tending the spread of sensitivity like the fire in winter's camp.

It's then that the vision fills with movement and color: the clan, with the play of naked, unfrightened children, busy looms, the carving of designs on pottery while the great heron's call. There are blondes among the laughing toddlers, and the Healing Woman's reddened hair mimics the darting flames in her blue eyes. The lines on her face flow the same course as the water marks on river rock, the etched patterns in her bone talismans, the waterfall twist of her walking staff.

I am soft in her presence, like quietly shifting sand. Open and vulnerable. I seek to deserve her council, deserve to be a conscious limb of the Goddess. Made worthy not only by our intent, but the impeccable manifestations of our love. We pledge to stand in ceremonial circle when we make our decisions, to spare no one our honest feelings. Pledged always to follow our mystical insight with direct personal action, yet never to forget the spiritual heart of this vital resistance, our sacrament . . .

We struggle, win or lose, because it is right to do so, because to do anything less than everything possible is not enough. Because we are part of the dis-ease unless we become part of the cure. Because we can't live with ourselves unless we act, righteously, whole heartedly, the impassioned champions of life, freedom, diversity, magic . . .

This is our true worth, our real value as individuals, our lives manifesting the art of sacred resistance, a perfect dance. A ghost dance not just to halt the immediate destruction, but to call back the bison and jaguar and the vistas of the chest-high prairie grasses.

We're not really winning in the present time. Our victories are morale boosting but always temporary. We are winning in the long run, in the flex of spirit, the surge of evolution, the dauntless will of creation to continue living, changing, expressing itself in countless new forms, forever!

We *are* winning. Spirit *is* winning. Measured in geologic time, patriarchal techno-humanity is only a brief outbreak, a spasm of imbalance and a masterpiece of satire.

No one will cry harder than I will at the death of the last condor, of the last grizzly bear, the impoundment of the last wild river. But that spiritual continuum of which we are a permanent part, that expanse of awareness that is the very breath of the living Goddess Earth—as a part of all that we will survive to hear the bone-crushing sounds of newly-evolved carnivores imparting alertness to their prey. As a part of creation, we will survive to see bridges deteriorate and abandoned dams washed to the sea by rivers running free again. Thought and action rejoined in a common effort. The old woman twists our resisting minds around to show us *all* sides of the Goddess. Not only creative, but destructive. A world ceaselessly consuming itself, forever in the process of "becoming." Giant floods as well as trickling streams, tornadoes faithfully following the kiss of summer's breeze. She is not only innocent and pure, but wantonly sexual and a ravaging killer. Not only an ancient crone, but a stretching newborn, quick to heal and quick to forget.

She is love and life. *Vida*, but also *muerta*, the thing that humans fear most in the dark symbols of wilderness—the imposing meaninglessness of their seemingly brief lives, the black reaches of their death . . .

Healing Woman teaches us that nothing leaves, no soul departs to septic golden halls or into another human form. She tells how our spirit-energy feeds back into the continuum we never really left. Dancing in place. Crazy Horse said "It's a good day to die," and could in that way live life to its fullest. Or my Nordic ancestors' embrace of the Valkyries, warrior maidens that accompany the fallen man or woman gone "Viking" against the creeping monoculture. No longer "creator" and "created," only the "all" and the "everything." Her stare settles on me in this rarefied air of possibility. . .

The "hawksfell" that holds this skald's pen also carries the tools of the warrior to wrench "wound-dew" from the rapist machine, "feed the ravens" with their inequity, "sate the eagles" with vanquished despoilers and the convulsions of my own sacrificed heart.

Fragments . . . I bend over again to gather up the particles of crumbled rock, and surprise! The stone made whole! It fits snugly in my sling once more.

May I never breathe a single lungful, nor enter into any struggle without this voiceless litany.

No fragmentation. No temptation to retreat. No reasons to regret.

I often wake up when the birds rustle at first light. I stare in blissful wordlessness at the fading stars through the opening of my medicine cave, wait for the earliest spears of sunshine to pierce the purple and vermilion Kachina cliffs, total love's fatal thrust . . .

The Returning Storm

NACHTWERKE: Nightwork; Ed Abbey's definition of social responsibility.

RESPONSIBILITY: The ability to respond.

> "Rest assured, Yellow Wolf. It will only get
> more difficult for you."
> — the response I received
> from a Mayan Shaman

Finally, even those conformist
handmaidens of society
will know something is going on
in the untamed "out there."
The returning storm of Bio-Diversity,
rising like dust-clouds
kicked up by a battle in progress;
like smoke signals, swollen
into the flesh of destiny,
turning despair into a joyous anger.

This mind is on fire.
The words which escape
its lockerful of secrets
are the staccato bursts
of boiling electrolite.

Press a cool hand to this forehead,
the relief of a waterfall
moving beneath it.

Blow on this anxious face,
the relief of dancing winds—
the returning storm now whipping away
the hissing steam
 where fire meets water . . .

"The mountains glower at us," she wrote,
". . . shame us for our distance."
"A rosy barb beneath yellow fur,"
what some would call love,
not without pain.

Now making love
at the gate of Mayan-Tibetan-Hopi prophesy.
No garment can conceal
such Kokopellic excitement.
Multiple shadows from the flute-wrench,
cast by a candle that burns on both ends,
delivering the songs of the committed.

The footprints are
all too easily identifiable,
still flaming,
leading to the smashed cages
of grandfather Condor,
liberated, lusting Wolves,
sensual Mt. Lions,
and a She-Bear—
free once again
to make mischief with the Earth.

WHO'LL TELL IT TO THE CHILDREN?

We often fight the symptoms of our global sickness without coming to terms with their common cause, our deliberate divorce from the sacred Mother Earth, our source. Children not taught the equality and sanctity of the rest of creation grow into pitiful adults arguing over selfish "management plans."

Nuclear war, discrimination, acid rain, water pollution, prejudice, the relocation of native traditionalists, our government's latest funding of right-wing dictators—all mere symptoms of our "dis-ease." Our disenchantment, our voluntary separation from the harmonic totality from which we arose.

Sticking barbwire fences in her sides, we fence in our own potential. Covering her with asphalt, we concrete over our own spontaneity, our own freedom. Blasting holes into her bowels, we suck out the black blood of those animals we would follow into extinction. Displease the spirits.

Who'll tell it to the children when they ask why there's no wild allowed inside of them, no wilderness left for them to save? Who'll tell it to the children?

It is not enough to hide in the cities, lost in liberal intellectualization, voting in established environmental groups for our vacationland acreage. It's not enough to meditate, to be "New Age," to eat organic, while the last sacred places, places of power, are destroyed forever.

The future is in the hands of the little "wolves." May they never stop howling! Help the children. Help them feel the undammed rivers that flow through their veins, feel the mountains in their hearts; go from compassion to passion. To *insist* on wilderness, *insist* on their dance. To avoid compromise, to be real, to be natural. To experience with every one of their senses their vital connection to the living God-force, to the sacred Mother

Let our *action* be our prayer. Let all that's good come from our prayer.

The Woodpecker Riff

At the onset of global transformation,
intellectualization is not enough.
In a world of cold automatons,
empathy remains insufficient.

For unwavering separateness,
you are awarded as many miles between us
as you need for your perceived comfort.

For your resolute distance,
you are awarded as many centuries apart
as you need to stop fearing.

At the sound of your silent scream,
the woodpecker returns to its tree;
still knocking its head against
the hardened crusts
that encase our consciousness.

Follow his feather down to where I lie,
there, at the base of giant
vine-covered statues of the great mystery.
Hairy legs up in the air
blowing the blues harp
with a cocky grin on my face!

From time to time you'll feel this wildest music
invade your hesitant feet,
as you rhythmically travel
each vanishing year of your life.

This celebratory riff,
echoing on subconscious waves
across the safe and sterile expanses between us,
is my way of supporting your individual dance,
my way of continuing to touch you . . .
Freed from an inexplicable emptiness,
by the invigorating winds of the Muse!

THE BOTTOM LINE

Gary said, "Get to the bottom line!"

This is the bottom line . . . it is all cultures reaching back to the tribal roots we share in common. Root humanity, primal humanity—gazing out of dark caves in the Mother Earth, the womb, out over crackling fires to the rivers and mountains where eyesight fails and vision takes over. Always alert, always in awe of the mysteries behind the clouds, behind the illusions of mortality and reality, reverent of the spirit in all of creation. The flickering firelight makes the trees and rocks appear alive, and indeed they are! Life in water, wind, plants and animals. Each sings a unique presence, and yet all harmonize as individual expressions of the same being: our Earth Mother. This is the Sacred Circle, the living religion of the ancestors of Celts, Vikings, Visigoths . . . It is the so-called barbarian world-view which still threatens the sterile manifestations of logos. The ego-centric mind barricades itself against sensitivity and nature, erecting walls like Rome against the barbarians of the forests. It is a mind-view still practiced by indigenous peoples in touch with the earth, people who are called savages in many modern tongues. This living of life as if all creation mattered, as if the Earth were our mother's flesh, is our common spiritual history. Now called "Deep Ecology," whereby contemporary humanity re-learns how to live with sensitivity and reverence on the land, protecting the remaining wildlands as outdoor chapels where our children, —laughing, beautiful children—can learn the lessons of the Great Spirit. Protected for their diversity, untamed, unmanaged, not just for the benefit of our species, but because every element of nature, every living being has an equal right to dance out its destiny unfettered, free . . .

Even fools step softly when they recognize it's

their mother they step on. Right living. From the radical defense of wilderness exemplified by our heartfelt struggle, to the inspired poetry, music and art that slap the blinders off and open the heart. No East or West—conservative or liberal. The only view that matters is that which transcends *all* differences, that celebrates the magic and diversity of creation, that heralds a return to the untamed wilds, to the wild potential within us all: The View of Spirit. The return, Full Circle— *LOVE* . . .

WOLF-KACHINA

This all happens at the indefinite edge of dawn, where it's easy to mistake reflected starlight or the subdued glow of our dreams for the break of day. The tall shadows of piñon sway back and forth in moon-crazed winds, concealing his prancing steps. Dried up pine cones blow melodically across the forest floor, indistinguishable from the chuckles rising from his throat. We hear each tiny noise from a world waking up, precursors of things to come.

We look through narrowed eyes with an intensity heightened by our fear: a brief glint of light on his painted gourd rattle. An illusion of sparks wherever he lifts his feet from the hallowed ground. What's this? The smell of his wet fur is known to bring barren does into heat; known to keep boys and girls awake at night with visions that expand, like the stretching womb, to encompass the future . . .

Even in the dark,
his fertile member rises like a parable
no one can forget.

Even in the dark,
truth is a starved wolf, ready to cull the sick
and weak minds.

Even the strongest of us—
warrior women and men, warrior children—
are repeatedly tested by truth's implications.

We are frayed at the edges, but the center is intact. It is in the center that we tend the sacred fire, straighten our arrows, conceive on its sensual furs the progeny of our collective spirit. Surviving each exhaustive dance in our progression,

151

we prove we can be shattered and centered at the same time. Destroyed and recreated.

Dancing, he comes.
His howls are the sound of blood over bone,
a descendant of the moon.

Dancing, he comes.
There is no calling him,
there is no stopping him.

Dancing, he comes.
Setting off every trap,
without ever getting caught.

Dancing, he comes.
Ripping into our preconception, our habit,
pride, mechanical addictions . . .

Dancing, he comes.
Licking the sockets of our eyes
with raspy tongue
until we can see with our guts,
see with our hearts.

"Yes," he would tell us, if only we knew how to listen, "when there is no storm, I am the power that so rudely blows the hair out from in front of your eyes." But his calm demeanor leads us to believe he has no designs on these virginal daughters of cognition. He is the mystery that challenges our preconception, the security of our world-view, and our most guarded thoughts.

We needn't think of White Buffalo Woman as sexless, chaste, untouched . . . It's just that her lust is for the manifestations of magic. Spirit entered her, in its entirety, and so nothing else can satisfy.

Indeed!

The hair on our arms ripples in the pre-dawn darkness. It signals the arrival of Wolf-Kachina, one of the emissaries of the Great Spirit.

And before full light, he will dance past all our cerebral defenses, hungrily devour our arrogant sense of certainty . . . make wild, abandoned love to the pubescent offspring of perception.

Wolf-River

"People like you help
 people like me go on."
                          — Si Kahn

I am a river.
I wear away with my intensity
the rough boundaries that would contain me.

I am ever-changing
yet always the same.
None fully understand my complexities,
so I am alternately lusted for and feared.

Cultures and religions
spring from my fertile banks;
mystery flowers
and myth is fused to reality.

I can both heat you and cool you.
I am the real meaning of "wet dreams"—
experience my flow.

Leap into my movement
and I will touch you everywhere at once
I will enter your openings
and exhilarate you.

The dampness you hide in public
is me calling you.

I howl down ancient Indian canyons,
endlessly pursuing freedom
like a fleeing deer.
I wash away dams and aluminum trailers—
mere child's play!
My wet sounds are the soundtrack
for lovers, tree-huggers,
and the rapid movements of duck wings.

Your love and appreciation
are blossoms tossed into my swirling waters.
They tickle my Wolf-River belly,
touch my most hidden secrets.

I'll carry your gifts with me:
my friend's firm support and lover's abandon.
I'll fondle the petals,
sniff its persistent musk.
If you are far away, and hear
a roaring in your ears,
it is I, Wolf-River, loving you back . . .

Patience

Becca wrote:
"Draw the patience of the stones and rocks
into yourself,
that you might share their patience
in having your dreams fulfilled.

"I ache for my visions, so vivid,
shining with sweat,
filling me with their sweet smells
and bursting desire.

Like a wolf caged,
I leap against the bars
of alleged reality,
until they give way
to freedom and fantasy.

I ache for my visions,
the way they throw me on my back,
roughly undress me,
plant feathers in my skin,
and toss me off the cliffs.

I taste fear like metal on my tongue,
until my body drains out through my nuts,
and I become wind . . .

I ache for my visions, so vivid . . .

THE FUTURE-PRIMITIVE

I can only relate it to you in dream-time. A million stars in blackest sky. Cedar smoke wafts out into the ether from this womb-like cave-kiva-rock home. Smells of sage and copal clear the mind. The smells of fur on the floor, children playing, adult sex glands. The strength of the clan is here, an invisible web that connects us wordlessly to each other. There, by the fire, you squat, sharpening arrows against a stone's raspy sides, each motion a fluid haiku. You are more than a spirit-warrior. You are Mother Earth herself when she takes the form of a two-legged. Unknown to the others, I can see you without looking your way, and you see me without looking up from your wooden shafts, deftly rolled like a sexual poetry.

Feathers flap from coup sticks, carved for touching into Viking-Tibetan-Mayan-Anasazi figures intertwined. We have each proved our worth by this time, worthy to enjoy the miracle of life, of awareness. Yet still they know me to be different. The horned-one of the Eylesean caves in Paleolithic France, excused for his lack of manners, his fanciful lack of restraint. Pan, following your scent trail with a mischievous grin. The persistent Kokopelli, horned flute player who, no matter how heavy the load, maintains his dance. They imagine an excess of fur on my body, a rippling in liquid flesh they interpret as danger. Yet I have their respect, for I came as foretold in the dreams of the elders, in the cryptic toss of crystals at the foot of rainforest pyramids. They know that, like Buffalo people and Jaguar women, the Wolf beings are an asset to the new tribe. Somehow carrying in their defiance the power for the evolution of spirit. They keep the gates of perception open with the strength of their stare.

So they allow me my grating certainty, the distant voices that make for my alone times. Unlike people before the testing, these allow me the unsettling visions that only you share.

It is here, in the future-primitive, that we can truly know ourselves. It is here we find each other. Returning to ancient ways of "seeing" to carry on the seeds of evolving consciousness. Here, the women too are armed, confidence like spears in their hands. The children's every movement is a choreography of their nimble power.

The children learn early to feel the pain of the deer and the correct way to give thanks; position the head just so, spread cornmeal before the mouth, see through the eyes of the deer. And to hear the cries of the plants pulled from our garden next to the river, give thanks for each life absorbed into our life, no matter how small. They find clever uses for scraps and remnants of the age of technology, a piece of mesh for a fire-grate, a section of soul-less PVC pipe salvaged for makeshift canteen beneath the shadow of eagle feathers.

By not fearing death, we will have found the power to cure ourselves. Free to act out our destiny, because we're free to move on into the great flux of life, feeding the buzzards and the plants, feeding back into life's spiritual grid. The illusion of separateness falls away in the time of trial. It is time to re-empower ourselves, time to set out the prayer-sticks.

The fall of Babylon is not the end of life. The nuclear storms of the dark gods Teacatlipoca and Huitzilopochtli are not the end of life. The collapse of Tula and Teotihuacan occurs first inside each warrior's heart, then again in the shredding of industrial civilization. The exciting feel of Quetzalcoatl, the feathered-serpent within us. Writhing passion!

Let those who dare be the seeds! Seeds of consciousness, of love, of change. A time for the few to come together and line their high-mountain nests with the physical and spiritual aids to survival. Time to ignore no lessons, ignore no enemy, ignore no ally . . .

Let those who dare be the seeds. I touch you from across our fire-lit shelter. You touch back without turning, arranging the prayer-sticks in a way that points the direction we must travel—together . . .

LoneWolfCircles   Gila Wilderness '80

MANIFESTING THE DREAM

"To All My Relations . . ."

> — Amerindian prayer, referring to not only other people, but to the trees, animals, rocks . . .

"It seems to me an artificial boundary to keep spirituality and politics separate . . . Because they are so inextricably interwoven into all aspects of our lives, our spiritual traditions are the very foundation of our political actions . . . To those exhorting me to 'visualize world peace' in order to cure the ills of the world, I say, can I simply visualize food if my people are hungry, or visualize freedom when my people are oppressed? To those telling me to 'turn the other cheek', I say no."

> — Mahtowin, Oglala Lakota Woman

Every struggle for a healthier, freer, more just world takes place behind the front lines of wilderness destruction. Industrial inhumanity meets paradise on the killing fields, at the farthest reaches of the "civilized" juggernaut. In the name of limitless growth, compulsive consumption, and our regulated comforts, it rolls on over the last wild places. Diverse life is crushed beneath it, along with freedom, spontaneity, indigenous cultures and those well-meaning reformers co-opted into tossing themselves under its grinding wheels.

This is the emergency ward, hurriedly set up in a makeshift camp in the shrinking "DMZ." The wilderness assault is a vanguard action. All other injustices occur inside these newly secured lines.

We rush to where the soulless, metal serpent strikes. We leap between it and beloved wilderness, often catching the fangs in our own bodies instead, but countless heads will strike again and again until we confront the unified "nature" of the beast, or it suffocates from the accumulative pressure of its own ponderous bulk.

Radical ecology is ecology armed. It is a spiritual ecology that recognizes the complex social mechanics of environmental destruction. It is consciousness of Earth's inclusive needs. It is spirited resistance, love, commitment and the will to escalate our conscious involvement.

Deep ecology is an exercise rooted in the tribal cultures of our prehistory. It is the interactive awareness of the Earth—the Earth as a living organism. This "sacred world view" predates and was supplanted by systems of repression. If humans survive to ponder civilization's sordid downfall, they will find precisely this perspective, this awareness, again insuring the liveability, diversity and natural fulfillment of all creation.

Radical deep ecology is a recent outgrowth, drawing from thousands of years of Earth consciousness and of social revolutionary thought, responding to an unprecedented pandemic crisis. The insistent spark of the shaman is reborn in the ecological activist doing the dance of resistance against overwhelming odds, bloodied poets of the wilderness Golgotha. It is the cutting edge of revolutionary spirit, tempered in the blood of lifeforms sacrificed to our "humanity," sharpened by the raspy truths of social vivisection and tested by the precepts of eco-feminist response.

Radical ecology demands we act on our awareness. Doing anything less than you possibly can is not enough! In the face of selfish, wholesale slaughter, inaction is synonymous with complicity. We free up our wild inner nature in the process of emancipating "external" nature. It only appears "radical" against the backdrop of banal contemporary society, which considers any act of conscience extreme, any personal risk too high, any discomfort too much to bear. This ecology is an ecosophy of practice.

Unmanipulated nature is beyond both hierarchy and anarchy. It is expressed in the subtle patterns of flow, of life consuming itself in such a way as to never diminish any one part of itself. Nature is a feeding frenzy, an orgy of experience—yet if we could step back from our place in it we would see the cohesive masterpiece these swirling colors create. There is no chaos, no anarchy—only unperceived patterns. Nature is form without constraint, purpose without order, design without limit, kinetic and complete.

> "To the extent that we perceive boundaries we fall short of deep ecological consciousness."
>
> — Warwick Fox

Radical ecologists and spiritual ecologists share the recognition of borders as indefensible constructs. Bioregions and international boundaries are incompatible. They are part of the compartmentalization of our experience. Rectangular blocks full of square houses, with occupants who work in square factories and every moment of whose lives is measured in an inflexible concept of time. We cannot accept the legitimacy of borders, or any other abstract symbol of dominion, measurement, segregation, or human manipulation.

We face a unified threat, a many-headed Kraken, Gisnberg's "Molloch," expressed, defined, and enforced by schools, factories, police, courts, Forest Service, border patrol. Each acts to guarantee production, uniformity and obedience. We barely skirt hypocrisy when we condemn the Forest Service for its abhorrent cutting practices; yet, grant them a charter to officiate over token exclusionary wilderness.

Aldo Leopold wrote, "There are woods that are plain to look at, but not to look into," teaching that to really *see* magnificence is as much a measure of the viewer as it is of the view. Site-specific protection of officially designated "wilderness" (which we call "pristine," "unique," "beautiful") implies that everywhere else is somewhat *less* special, hence open to development and defilement. Our support for a system of limited wilderness "reservations" weakens the continuity of the biological fabric, as surely as the system of Indian reservations unravels the cultural cohesion of native America. The result is ecological statism.

Evolution cannot rely on isolated pockets of wilderness as genetic preserves. Life there represents a shrinking gene pool, marginalized by boundaries, threatened with extinction. Additionally, the rapid build-up of hydrocarbons in the atmosphere (the "greenhouse effect") is resulting in climatic shifts that may trigger the extinction of current endangered species, or force their migration from their legislated enclaves.

Furthermore, revolutionary and evolutionary mandates—tens of thousands years of indefeasible human yearning—demand more of us. To narrow the focus and isolate our efforts while accepting the basic authority of the patriarchal state is to embrace that very beast which is even now robbing the life and dignity of wild Earth. *Radical* deep ecology, on the other hand, insists we cease giving our tacit consent, withdraw all participation from the destructive system.

I am in no way suggesting we slack off on our efforts to salvage the remaining wilderness, only that we aren't foolish enough to settle for that. We insist on "Big Wilderness" which retains the integrity of entire ecosystems, includes wilderness corridors to accommodate potential migrations, and encompasses enough area to encourage *every* species' celebratory dance. "Survival," either for other plants and animals or for us, is not enough. All life deserves the fruits of its three-and-a-half billion year adventure, to really *live*—that fullest experiencing of sensation, freedom, and innate self. "Wildlife" are not really wild inside gulag zoos and preserves, not really "themselves." In the same way, we cannot satisfy our "first nature" or fulfill the potential of our primal beings within the walls of nameless cities and confines of the social experience. We are freest, most "ourselves," in direct interaction with the raw processes of nature—wary, sensitized, wide awake. Urbanization and domestication of humankind are penance to our dictatorial left-brains, the analytical-categorical-logical side that makes squares of circles, hells out of paradise, sin out of pleasure, misery out of crafts, schedules of the adventure of the moment, time out of the timeless, competition out of love. It impounds open estuaries and free-flowing passages into canal locks for commerce, makes little compartments out of the vast cerebral plains, standardizes definitions for infinite possibility. It solidifies change, reduces action to debate, pretends to limit the limitless.

Those people closest to the Earth, its rhythms, its secrets—the hunter-gatherers, curanderas, and shamans of a hundred different cultures—know nothing of the realities of nuclear war or global, incurable plagues. Yet they all speak of an imminent cleansing, of the Earth's unhurried self-regulation, of revolution and cataclysm. We arrogantly sit in the technological bubble, imagine ourselves somehow removed from the ill effects of our paradigm and the tumultuous throes of an Earth in transition. Primal peoples know what civilized "man" has forgot: we are all an integral part of this living planet, humans will suffer the pain they inflict on other parts of the Earth-body, and this Earth-body will go on manifesting spirit in evolutionary flowering with or without either the rationalist diatribes or poetic indulgences of human witness.

> "Civilization is like a sick man, down for so long he is unable to smell the stench of his own death."
> — Chief Sealth

The requirements of a pampered humanity have always come first, at the expense of all other lifeforms and, finally, to the detriment of humans themselves. The Earth isn't going to allow that anymore. The processes of oppression and ecological devastation are implemented along social, political and class lines, requiring our analysis and attention. Doctrinal comparisons, however, are exhaustive and moot debated at the precipitous brink of our extinction.

We see the dire results of each purely technological "cure" everywhere we look obstructing our view, surrounding us, suffocating us. The disastrous nuclear industry was launched as a "clean alternative" to other power sources. Civilization, in its greyest, most repressing incarnations, is the product of history, "his-story." It is the enforced paradigm of the victor—the expediter, the controller, the manipulator, the legislator, the eradicator . . .

We need "visualization," but we also need revision, re-evolution, and manifestation. It is clean mountain water, not visualization of it, that refreshes the face and satisfies the thirst. The immediate future will be a painful and traumatic rewriting of the dominant paradigm, not "history" this time, but *her*-story, in an irrevocable and dramatic telling.

We have the free-will option to be the dam on the river, or an active participant in the flood that removes it: the deliberate, heartfelt, uncompromised excising of the industrial leviathan.

It gave us color TV, and imposed a black and white world. It promises we can "have fun," but "don't be late," "get dirty," or do anything unplanned. It promises time to play, but only a toxic, concrete playground. Participate! Do something unplanned! Stay late. Get dirty. Replant the playground. Tear up the concrete. Recreate the wild, while you celebrate it!

"Beneath the ash, the ash of pavement, lies the certainty of seed." The answer, again, is found in nature.

The Pan-American highway is a sterile imposition, covering a diverse terrain with stifling monotony. But down near the equator, the abundant rain and incredible heat of the sun accelerate the natural growth of plantlife. This multi-billion dollar technological investment requires constant repair, as insistent rainforest flora force their way up through the asphalt. The road departments' nightmare is the joyous expression of being!

Think of the relatively few awakened activists as persistent, adaptive, struggling green shoots. Rooted. Growing. Spreading out, flexing beneath the festering asphalt. It's a little dark under here, but still obvious which way is up, and what it is that holds us down.

Listen! Listen to the first loud cracks in the pavement! They set the tempo for the canyon songbird's call: Arriba! Arriba! Arriba!

Arise!

This Is The Way

My vision began with words
under the shifting weight
of mortality.

But then I wake up from busy-ness,
tired,
and my head falls off.

Laying down,
my body becomes an ocean,
evaporating.

Freed by the sun,
I return
to the eyes of the animals.

Colored rock,
seaweed, cactus fruit,
and a view of the clouds.

This is the way
the wind fills me,
where I am no more.

APPENDIX

RECOMMENDED READING

Periodicals:

The Trumpeter	Victoria, BC, Canada
Creation	P.O. Box 19216,
	Oakland, CA 94619
Earth First! Journal	P.O. Box 5176,
	Missoula, MT 59806
Talking Leaves	1430 Willamette St.,#367,
	Eugene, OR 97401
Wild Earth	P.O. Box 492,
	Canton, NY 13617
Buzzworm	P.O. Box 6853,
	Syracuse, NY 13217
Katuah Journal	P.O. Box 638,
	Leicester, NC 28748
High Country News	P.O. Box 1090,
	Paonia, CO 81428

Books:

Sacred Land, Sacred Sex by Dolores LaChapelle
   (Finn Hill Arts)
Deep Ecology by Bill Devall & George Sessions
   (Gibbs M. Smith, Inc.)

Simple in Means, Rich in Ends by Bill Devall
   (Gibbs M. Smith, Inc.)
The Great Cosmic Mother by Barbara Mor
   & Monica Sjoo
   (Harper & Row Pubs., Inc.)
Spiritual Ecology by Jim Nollman
   (Bantam New Age)
Green Rage by Christopher Manes
   (Little, Brown & Co.)
The Practice of the Wild by Gary Snyder
   (Northpoint)

Plus any titles by the following:

Terry Tempest Williams
Starhawk
Gary Snyder
Barry Lopez
Paul Sheperd
Peter Mathiesson
Joseph Campbell

STAY IN TOUCH

On the following pages you will find listed, with their current prices, some of the books and tapes now available on related subjects. Your book dealer stocks most of these, and will stock new titles in the Llewellyn series as they become available. We urge your patronage.

However, to obtain our full catalog, to keep informed of new titles as they are released and to benefit from informative articles and helpful news, you are invited to write for our bi-monthly news magazine/catalog. A sample copy is free, and it will continue coming to you at no cost as long as you are an active mail customer. Or you may keep it coming for a full year with a donation of just $5.00 in U.S.A. & Canada ($20.00 overseas, first class mail). Many bookstores also have *The Llewellyn New Times* available to their customers. Ask for it.

Stay in touch! In *The Llewellyn New Times'* pages you will find news and reviews of new books, tapes and services, announcements of meetings and seminars, articles helpful to our readers, news of authors, advertising of products and services, special money-making opportunities, and much more.

The Llewellyn New Times
P.O. Box 64383-347, St. Paul, MN 55164-0383, U.S.A.
• • •
TO ORDER BOOKS AND TAPES

If your book dealer does not have the books and tapes described on the following pages readily available, you may order them directly from the publisher by sending full price in U.S. funds, plus $1.50 for postage and handling for orders *under* $10.00; $3.00 for orders *over* $10.00.

There are no postage and handling charges for orders over $50. UPS Delivery: We ship UPS whenever possible. Delivery guaranteed. Provide your street address as UPS does not deliver to P.O. Boxes. UPS to Canada requires a $50 minimum order. Allow 4-6 weeks for delivery. Orders outside the U.S.A. and Canada: Airmail—add retail price of book; add $5 for each non-book item (tapes, etc.); add $1 per item for surface mail.

FOR GROUP STUDY AND PURCHASE

Because there is a great deal of interest in group discussion and study of the subject matter of this book, we feel that we should encourage the adoption and use of this particular book by such groups by offering a special "quantity" price to group leaders or "agents."

Our Special Quantity Price for a minimum order of five copies of *Full Circle* is $38.85 cash-with-order. This price includes postage and handling within the United States. Minnesota residents must add 6 1/2% sales tax. For additional quantities, please order in multiples of five. For Canadian and foreign orders, add postage and handling charges as above. Credit card (VISA, Master Card, American Express) orders are accepted. Charge card orders only may be phoned free ($15.00 minimum order) within the U.S.A. or Canada by dialing 1-800-THE-MOON. Customer service calls dial 1-612-291-1970. Mail Orders to:

LLEWELLYN PUBLICATIONS
P.O. Box 64383-347 / St. Paul, MN 55164-0383, U.S.A.

THE GAIA TRADITION
by Kisma K. Stepanich

The Gaia Tradition provides a spiritual foundation upon which women, from all walks of life, can stand, finding support and direction. It is an eclectic blend of Wicca, Native American Spirituality and Dianic Goddess worship. Author Kisma Stepanich guides the reader to spiritual attunement with Mother Earth—through the evolution of the Goddess within, and through connection to the Goddess without.

The Gaia Tradition describes the Goddess philosophy and takes us month by month, season by season, through magical celebrations of the Goddess. The book includes valuable information for the avid ritualist/ ceremonialist and lists 2,000 names and origins of the Goddess from diverse cultures.

Stepanich shares her own experiences, poems and blessings, and stresses a woman's spiritual tradition that is not anti-male; rather calls for balance of the male/female energies. Through a series of lessons that deal with beliefs, deep ecology, rituals, spells and more, *The Gaia Tradition* helps women take a more dignified stance in their everyday lives and begin walking the path of whole and self-assured individuals.

0-87542-766-9, 336 pgs., 6 x 9, photos, illus.   **$12.95**

Llewellyn's MOON SIGN BOOK

It's not hard to see why *Llewellyn's Moon Sign Book* has become one of the world's favorite almanacs—it's fun, informative and has been a great help to millions in their daily planning; it's a complete guide to yearly living! The cycles of the Moon can and do affect everything from planting to buying a car. The best dates for any activity—gardening, fishing, hunting, building, repairing, moving, investing, buying and selling and more—are featured here. Published annually since 1906, *Llewellyn's Moon Sign Book* gives you all of the information you need in order to make the most of these natural cycles in easy-to-use tables and the famous "Astro-Almanac."

The Moon has a profound effect on our lives, and its precise influence is explained by the insightful articles by prominent forecasters and writers in the fields of gardening, astrology, politics, economics and cycles. From home, family and pets; leisure and recreation; health and beauty; business, finance and legal; farm and garden; to world events, *Llewellyn's Moon Sign Book* explores practically everything under the Moon!

State year   **$4.95**

THE GODDESS CALENDAR
Paintings by Hrana Janto

Enthusiasm for the Goddess in all her manifestations builds year by year. We published our first Goddess calendar in 1991, and sold more than 13,000 copies. Our 1992 and 1993 calendars are no exception. Full-color originals are done by artist Hrana Janto in a soft but powerful style. Her paintings express the many faces of the Goddess, and are created using different layers of media.

The 1992 calendar features goddesses from around the world including: Rhiannon (Wales), Morgan Le Fay (Celt), Nut (Egypt), Skadi (Scandinavia), Yemaya (Africa), Sophia (Judeo-Christian), Artemis and Demeter (Greece), Inanna (Sumer), Tara (Tibet) Estsanatlehi (Navajo), Pachamama (Peru), and Amaterasu (Japan). The 1993 calendar will bring Pele, Bloudewedd, White Buffalo Woman, Aphrodite, Oya, Vila, Maeve, Ix Chel, Oestre, Sarasvati, Nu Kwa, Tanith and Sedna to the enchanting pages of the calendar.

The Goddess Calendar makes a beautiful addition to any room. Each Goddess and her symbolism is clearly described month by magical month. Plus the date pages include important holiday information and Moon phases. Hrana Janto's powerful use of pastels makes it an an excellent gift for any occasion.

Born into a family of artists, Hrana Janto received her Bachelor of Fine Arts from the Cooper Union School of Art. Her many commissioned works include 12 illustrations for the PBS series "The Power of Myth" with Joseph Campbell and Bill Moyers; book covers for the Chelsea Book series "Monsters of Mythology"; and illustrations for *The Snake Princess*.

1992 Calendar, 0-87542-469-4, 24 pgs., 12 x 13, full-color
1993 Calendar, 0-87542-904-1, 24 pgs., 12 x 13, full-color

THE BOOK OF GODDESSES & HEROINES
by Patricia Monaghan

The Book of Goddesses & Heroines is a historical landmark, a must for everyone interested in Goddesses and Goddess worship. It is not an effort to trivialize the beliefs of matriarchal cultures. It is not a collection of Goddess descriptions penned by biased male historians throughout the ages. It is the complete, non-biased account of Goddesses of every cultural and geographic area, including African, Japanese, Korean, Persian, Australian, Pacific, Latin American, British, Irish, Scottish, Welsh, Chinese, Greek, Icelandic, Italian, Finnish, German, Scandinavian, Indian, Tibetan, Mesopotamian, North American, Semitic and Slavic Goddesses!

Unlike some of the male historians before her, Patricia Monaghan eliminates as much bias as possible from her Goddess stories. Envisioning herself as a woman who might have revered each of these Goddesses, she has done away with language that referred to the deities in relation to their male counterparts, as well as with culturally relative terms such as "married" or "fertility cult." The beliefs of the cultures and the attributes of the Goddesses have been left intact.

Plus, this book has a new, complete index. If you are more concerned about finding a Goddess of war than you are a Goddess of a given country, this index will lead you to the right page. This is especially useful for anyone seeking to do Goddess rituals. Your work will be twice as efficient and effective with this detailed and easy-to-use book.

0-87542-573-9, 421 pgs., 6 x 9, illus.   **$17.95**

EARTH MEMORY
by Paul Devereux

Ancient monuments are our "memory banks." Stonehenge, Machu Picchu, Serpent Mound, the Great Pyramid: these ancient sacred sites can still be used today as doorways to the earth energies and perennial knowledge that were harnessed by the original builders. *Earth Memory* provides a new and exciting means for deciphering the information locked in the landscape of ancient sacred sites. It is an interactive process between sacred places of remote antiquity and the human psyche.

Sacred sites are indeed greater than the sum of their parts and, as shown in *Earth Memory*, they lead us to face profound possibilities about the nature of our planet, of consciousness, of our inner selves, and the relationships between all of these.

Earth Memory includes ground-plan geometrical and metrological studies, symbolism, ancient astronomy, folklore, shamanism, nature religions, geomancy, astro-archaeology, and the study of unusual energy effects. These individual topics have been described before but never have their relationships been so illuminated. This is truly a holistic approach bringing together the science of archaeology and earth mysteries.

No techniques for unraveling ancient secrets are beyond the scope of the reader, who is invited to use the methods at any site of his or her choosing. The author emphasizes that "being and seeing" are as important as collecting the facts.

0-87542-188-1, 320 pgs., 6 x 9, photos, illus. $12.95

SACRED SITES
Edited by Frank Joseph

The United States abounds with natural and manmade locations of unique and profound spiritual powers. Largely unrecognized, they occur throughout North America, sometimes in our own back yards. The purpose of *Sacred Sites* is to acquaint readers with these domestic sites, to provide their physical description, define their numinous qualities and suggest simple rituals for tapping into their special energies.

Sacred Sites covers the spiritual as well as the physical aspects of many magical sites unknown to even adepts on the subject. The collection of outstanding contributing writers tell prospective visitors how to open themselves psychically and fine-tune their innate sensitivities to the ancient voices and lingering energies of each location. All of the sacred centers described are intimately known to our writers, most of whom live near the sites, and with which they have been personally acquainted for many years.

0-87542-348-5, 6 x 9, photos, maps

EARTH GOD RISING
by Alan Richardson

The Horned God is our oldest god, and his story can be heard in mythology from around the world. We can all expect to find something of the Horned God's spirit within our genes. It is part of our psychological and spiritual heritage, our magical roots.

Today, in an age that is witnessing the return of the Goddess in all ways and on all levels, the idea of one more male deity may appear to be a step backward. But along with looking toward the feminine power as a cure for our personal and societal ills, we must remember to invoke those forgotten and positive aspects of our most ancient God. He provides the balance needed in this New Age, and he must be invoked as clearly and as ardently as the Goddess to whom he is twin.

The book shows how to make direct contact with your own most ancient potentials, as exemplified by the Horned God and Goddess. Using the simplest of techniques, available to everyone in any circumstance, *Earth God Rising* illustrates how we can create our own mystery and bring about real magical transformations without the need for groups, gurus, or elaborate ceremonies.

0-87542-672-7, 218 pgs., 5 1/4 x 8, illus.　　　**$10.95**

THE SECRET OF LETTING GO
by Guy Finley

The Secret of Letting Go reveals the secret source of a brand-new kind of inner strength. Whether you need to let go of a painful heartache, a destructive habit, a frightening worry or a nagging discontent, this book shows you how to call upon your own hidden powers and how they can take you through and beyond any challenge or problem.

In the light of your new and higher self-understanding, emotional difficulties such as loneliness, fear, anxiety and frustration fade into nothingness as you happily discover they never really existed in the first place. *The Secret of Letting Go* is a pleasing balance of questions and answers, illustrative examples, truth tales, and stimulating dialogues that allow the reader to share in the exciting discoveries that lead up to lasting self-liberation. *The Secret of Letting Go* goes beyond any material of its time.

0-87542-223-3, 240 pgs., 5 1/4 x 8　　　**$9.95**

IN THE SHADOW OF THE SHAMAN
by Amber Wolfe

Presented in what the author calls a "cookbook shaman-ism" style, this book shares recipes, ingredients, and methods of preparation for experiencing some very ancient wisdoms—wisdoms of Native American and Wiccan traditions, as well as contributions from other philosophies of Nature, as they are used in the shamanic way. Wolfe encourages us to feel confident and free to use her methods to cook up something new, completely on our own. This blending of ancient formulas and personal methods represents what Wolfe calls *Aquarian Shamanism*.

In the Shadow of the Shaman is designed to communicate in the most practical, direct ways possible, so that the wisdom and the energy may be shared for the benefits of all. Whatever your system or tradition, you will find this to be a valuable book, a resource, a friend, a gentle guide and support on your journey. Dancing in the shadow of the shaman, you will find new dimensions of Spirit.

0-87542-888-6, 384 pgs., 6 x 9, illus. **$12.95**

BIRTH OF A MODERN SHAMAN
by Cynthia Bend and Tayja Wiger

This is the amazing true story of Tayja Wiger. As a child she had been beaten and sexually abused. As an adult she was beaten and became a prostitute. To further her difficulties she was a member of a minority, a Native American Sioux, and was also legally blind.

Tayja's courage and will determined that she needed to make changes in her life. This book follows her physical and emotional healing through the use of Transactional Analysis and Re-Birthing, culminating in the healing of her blindness by the Spiritualistic Minister Marilyn Rossner, through the laying on-of-hands.

Astrology and graphology are used to show the changes in Tayja as her multiple personalities, another problem from which she suffered, were finally integrated into one. Tayja has become both a shaman and a healer.

In *Birth of a Modern Shaman* there are powerful skills anyone can develop by becoming a shaman, the least of which is becoming balanced, at peace with the world around you, productive and happy. By using the techniques in this book you will move toward a magickal understanding of the universe that can help you achieve whatever you desire, and can help *you* to become a modern shaman.

0-87542-034-6, 272 pgs., 6 x 9, illus. **$9.95**

WICCA: A Guide for the Solitary Practitioner
by Scott Cunningham

Wicca is a book of life, and how to live magically, spiritually, and wholly attuned with Nature. It is a book of sense and common sense, not only about Magick, but about religion and one of the most critical issues of today: how to achieve the much needed and wholesome relationship with our Earth. Cunningham presents Wicca as it is today—a gentle, Earth-oriented religion dedicated to the Goddess and God. This book fulfills a need for a practical guide to solitary Wicca—a need which no previous book has fulfilled.

Here is a positive, practical introduction to the religion of Wicca, designed so that any interested person can learn to practice the religion alone, anywhere in the world. It presents Wicca honestly and clearly, without the pseudo-history that permeates other books. It shows that Wicca is a vital, satisfying part of twentieth century life.

This book presents the theory and practice of Wicca from an individual's perspective. The section on the Standing Stones Book of Shadows contains solitary rituals for the Esbats and Sabbats. This book, based on the author's nearly two decades of Wiccan practice, presents an eclectic picture of various aspects of this religion. Exercises designed to develop magical proficiency, a self-dedication ritual, herb, crystal and rune magic, recipes for Sabbat feasts, are included in this excellent book.
0-87542-118-0, 240 pgs., 6 x 9, illus.   **$9.95**

WHEEL OF THE YEAR: Living the Magickal Life
by Pauline Campanelli

If like most Pagans you feel elated from the celebrations of the Sabbats and hunger for that feeling during the long weeks between Sabbats, then *Wheel of the Year* can help you to put the joy of celebration and the fulfillment of magic into your everyday life.

The wealth of seasonal rituals and charms contained in *Wheel of the Year* are all easily performed with materials readily available, and are simple and concise enough that the practitioner can easily adapt them to work within the framework of his or her Pagan tradition. Learn how to perform fire magic in November, the best time to make magic wands and why, the ancient magical secrets of objects found on a beach, and the secret Pagan symbolism of Christmas tree ornaments.

Whether you are a newcomer to the Craft or found your way back many years ago, *Wheel of the Year* will be an invaluable reference book in your practical magical library. It is filled with magic and ritual for everyday life and will enhance any system of Pagan Ritual.
0-87542-091-5, 192 pp., 7 x 10, illustrated   **$9.95**